Never a Dull Moment in Africa

– Memoir of an intrepid life

Mac Mackenzie

NEVER A DULL MOMENT IN AFRICA
– Memoir of an intrepid life

Copyright © 2020 Mac Mackenzie

For information contact : macmackenzie47@gmail.com

Cover design by Nicole Bartels
ISBN: 978-1-71670-191-7

First Edition: August 2020

I wish to dedicate this book to
my extraordinary wife Catherine,
who kept pushing and inspiring me
to eventually put pen to paper.
Thank you my angel!

& to "Sparky",
the one who insisted that I get
this book published.
You are a true friend indeed!

"Start by doing what's necessary;
then, do what's possible;
and suddenly, you are doing the impossible."

Francis of Assisi

CONTENTS

i

Prologue

NEVER A DULL MOMENT IN AFRICA is inspired by true-life events and experiences. As a result it was deemed necessary to make use of pseudonyms to protect the innocent – and the not so innocent.

My name is "Mac Mackenzie". I was born and raised in our beloved country, South Africa. From an early age, my biggest fear in life was that I was going to die before I could get around to living my life to the fullest. As a result, I adopted the motto: "Life's journey is not to arrive at the grave safely in a well preserved body, but rather to skid in sideways, totally worn out, shouting, " *What a fucking ride!*"

I do not portray myself as some kind of "Rambo" character in the least. In retrospect, I'm just an average kind of fellow, with a huge appetite for anything challenging or adventurous by nature. What better place than Africa, where there is never a dull moment, particularly when you least expect it.

The story line of events and experiences depicted in this book is threaded together by an amazing sailing adventure my wife, "Catherine", and I shared by sailing halfway across the world on our own. Come with us and experience things you never imagined!

1

The Pains of Childhood

CLOSE YOUR EYES AND PICTURE a country so incredibly beautiful, mountains that stand majestically above rolling landscapes, grassy savannahs, lush forests, vast deserts, dazzling coastlines, and wildlife species of every description which live harmoniously in its natural splendor. A mosaic of magnificent treasures that is so diverse, yet so unique in all its forms that it takes your breath away. Welcome to South Africa - a land of unparalleled beauty and wonder.

It is home to a potpourri of ethnic cultures and a complex history that has shaped the country into what it is today. This is the country that I call home - a place where I was privileged in taking my first breath of air.

As if it were yesterday, I can still clearly remember how the neighborhood kids and I made our first skateboards from an old pair of roller skates, raced down the streets in soapbox carts we made from scraps of wood and wheels from discarded strollers, built tree houses which we called our secret forts and made slingshots from strips of inner car tubes attached to a yoke from a branch.

We weren't privy to cell phones, iPads, television, computer games and the likes thereof. Our world comprised of spending time in the outdoors, fishing, camping, swimming in rivers, flying home-made kites and just having fun. When we got up to mischief – which we certainly did, our parents would punish us by sending us to our rooms.

As far back as my little brain can remember, I always had a zest for life. It was almost like a little rabid mongrel which was constantly gnawing at me to get up to mischief. I suppose in hindsight, unknowingly, this is where the title of the book *"Never a Dull Moment"* actually came to life. In my vocabulary, the word *"dull"* didn't exist.

The *"Africa"* addition to the title simply came about due to the fact that all of my escapades, adventures and near death experiences *mostly* took place somewhere in Africa.

Before I get ahead of myself again, I'll share a tale or two of my childhood escapades, which will explain why I have always had this relentless fight against boredom in my life. I was probably around nine years old when this incident took place...

My mother never backed her old *Fiat 124 Special* into the garage after returning from the store. She always drove straight in, with just enough walking space between the front of her car and a huge, handmade wardrobe which stood on four legs, which was pushed up-against the front wall of the garage.

With my little brother and I seated in the back of the car, I can still vividly remember seeing the intense concentration in my mother's eyes each time she backed out of the garage. She had this unique ability to unhinge her head from her shoulders and turn her head 180 degrees facing backwards over her shoulder. That's when one of my many bright ideas struck me like a sudden bolt of lightning. I knew there and then that this was going to be a blockbuster!

Upon returning from the store, I immediately jumped into action. After rummaging through my fathers' workshop, I eventually found just what I was looking for. It was a heavy duty rope which measured almost the full length of the garage. I attached one end underneath the front bumper of my mothers' prized *Fiat* and the other end to one of the legs of this enormous wardrobe in front of her car.

The following day, with my brother and I seated on the back seat, my mother started the car, unhinged her head from her shoulders as usual and started backing out of the garage. Just as the back wheels of the car rolled down the concrete ramp in front of the garage, the rope pulled taught. With absolute concentration whilst backing out, my mother slowly stepped on the gas into the driveway. The next moment there was a sound like a roar of thunder, the wardrobe screeched along the concrete floor and out the garage. With a loud crash, the lumbering beast toppled over.

My mother got such a fright that her head rotated forward with lightening speed, and I was convinced she would suffer from whiplash for the rest of her life!

Due to the wardrobe smashing to the ground, she didn't see anything in front of her. This just compounded the terror she was experiencing.

In a state of absolute shock, my mother jumped out of the car forgetting to put the gear-stick into neutral. The car lunged backwards with a sudden jolt, almost jerking her head off for the second time. With legs trembling like jelly, she finally exited the car and made her way around to the front. That's when it finally dawned on her that her *beloved* son had engineered this hellish experience.

Knowing full well what my sentence would be, I jumped out of the car and took off running with my mother yelling behind me, "*Mac, I'm going to wring your neck, you little shit!*"

Needless to say, my pimple-spotted little butt got a good spanking when I eventually returned home that evening.

The moment was priceless, albeit at the price of my mothers' impaired mental health from that day forward.

Whilst on the topic of ropes, looking out of my second-floor bedroom window one day, an ingenious idea yet again came to mind. Overlooking the swimming pool in the back yard, I imagined how awesome it would be to zipline from my bedroom window and drop into the pool below.

I rushed out and rounded up my neighborhood friends to join me in an epic adrenaline rush. We found a generous length of rope, attached one end to the center support column of the window frame and the other end to a tree just beyond the swimming pool.

Using a salvaged wheel from a stroller, I removed the tire from the rim and fed the rope through it, fashioning a pulley of sorts. I attached a short piece of rope with a sawn-off broomstick to hang onto and tied the other end to our rudimentary home-made pulley.

With the engineering sorted, it was time to try this baby out. Due to the fact that I was the brainchild behind this grand idea, I had the privilege of having the first go.

Just as I had imagined, my idea worked like a charm.

This no doubt evoked intense excitement as to who would go next. After each of us had a turn ziplining into the pool, I naturally had to amplify things a tad.

I suggested the three of us zipline together and create an enormous water-bomb. The idea sounded awesome and everyone was onboard to take things to the next level.

One by one, we climbed out of my bedroom window and clung onto the piece of broomstick for dear life. Being the last one out, I shoved us away by pushing my feet against the wall. The rope immediately sagged under our combined weight, which in turn placed an enormous strain on the window frame. By the time we reached the middle of the rope, the window frame couldn't bear the strain any longer and ripped out of the wall.

It was as if things were happening in slow motion. I remember becoming weightless all of a sudden and the three of us falling out of the air into the pool. Thinking that the rope had snapped, I looked up at the house and all I could see was a big gaping hole in the wall where a window used to be.

My mother who had been reading in her bedroom at the time, heard the loud crash as the window frame ripped out of the wall and crashed into pieces on the paved patio below. In a state of absolute bewilderment, she ran outside to investigate what had taken place and that's when she saw the frame and glass spread all over the patio floor.

Unsure of what had taken place; she turned and looked at the three little faces in the pool staring back at her with eyes the size of saucers.

"What on earth happened here Mac?"

Realizing that a shit storm was on the horizon, my friends jumped out of the pool and took off running, leaving me there to face the music on my own.

With an innocent look on my face, I replied, *"Mom, we were just playing when we heard the window fall on the ground".*

"Mac, how can just playing cause the window to rip out of the house?" my mother asked with utter frustration in her voice.

Knowing full well that my little ass was going to get a good tanning, I replied teary eyed, *"We were just sliding down the rope into the pool. The next thing we knew, the rope had somehow pulled the window out. It really wasn't our fault".*

Lost for words and still in a state of utter shock, my mother turned and walked away, leaving this disaster zone for my father to sort out when he returned from work.

Thank God as I grew up over the years, I somehow learnt to harness my exuberant zest for life and utilize it in less destructive ways. This lead to me taking up action sports such as skydiving, abseiling, mountain biking, white water rafting – and the list goes on...

*"All you need is the plan, the road map,
and the courage to press on to your destination."*

Earl Nightingale

2

On a Sailboat with a Psychopath

I'VE PARTICIPATED IN a variety of water sports from early childhood, such as surfing, swimming, underwater hokey, snorkeling, wind surfing, scuba diving, water volleyball and spearfishing, but I've always yearned to go sailing out on the open ocean.

One day, my first wife, "Denise", and I decided to pay a visit to the Royal Cape Yacht Club in Cape Town, hoping we could somehow hook-up with someone and go out sailing, just to see what it feels like. After hanging around for a while looking at all the different sail boats, we went up to the yacht club foyer and scanned through several posts pinned up on a notice board. One of the posts read, "*Crew wanted for a yacht delivery in the Caribbean. Couple preferred. No experience necessary!*"

"Here's just the opportunity that we've been looking for," I said to Denise.

I immediately called the cell phone number on the advert and spoke to a woman by the name of Mary-Anne.

"Hi, my name is Mac. My wife Denise and I saw your post at the yacht club that you're looking for crew. Are the positions still available?" I enquired.

"Hi Mac, they sure are," she replied warmly.

"You probably would like to know more about it, so may I suggest that we meet at the yacht club and discuss everything in person with you guys?"

"We're already here if you guys can make it?" I enquired.

"No problem, we'll see you in a couple minutes."

Whilst we were waiting at the bar for them, in walked a well-tanned couple, probably in their late forties. The woman was rather slenderly built, with long strawberry blonde hair and the guy with her had this typical "Robinson Crusoe" look about him. He was wearing a wide-brimmed hat with shoulder length, silver-grey hair and beard.

I turned to Denise and said, "*I think that must be them.*"

They walked up to us when the women asked, "*are you perhaps Mac and Denise?*"

"Yip, that's us," I replied, standing up from my seat.

She stuck out her hand and said, "*Hi, I'm Mary-Anne and this is my partner, Charles.*"

We shook hands and took up seats at a little table near the bar. After we ordered a round of beers, we got chatting.

"*The timing couldn't have been better*" Mary-Anne stated. "*We had just left the yacht club after pinning the advert up on the notice board, when you called.*"

"*That IS good timing,*" I exclaimed. "*We're rather excited to hear what this is all about.*"

Mary-Anne did most of the talking, "*Charles and I deliver yachts for a living and are always in need of crew. In fact, we just arrived back two days ago after delivering a yacht in the Caribbean Islands. The company that we contract for has back-to-back orders from a yacht charter company in St. Maarten.*"

After taking a sip from her beer, she continued, "*The next yacht should be ready in about two weeks' time. So this is how it works; in exchange for your help, we'll provide all the meals whilst onboard. There aren't any wages and you guys have to purchase your own airline tickets to return back to South Africa.*"

"*Just so that you know, Denise and I don't have any sailing experience.*"

Charles replied to my statement, "*That's not a problem; we'll show you what to do. It's rather simple really.*"

13

"So what do our jobs actually entail?" I enquired.

"Each of us will stand watch at the helm for two hours at a time. We'll also take turns making supper every day. For the rest, it's each to their own," Mary-Anne replied.

"That sounds cool. By the way, Denise is a pretty damn good cook!" I added proudly.

"Great, I can't wait to taste your food," Charles added quickly, licking his chops.

"How long is the trip?" I asked

"Depending on the weather, it usually takes about three to four weeks. Would that be a problem for you guys?" Charles enquired.

Looking briefly at Denise, I answered, *"I'm sure we can work something out."*

It was clearly evident that they've done this many times before. Mary-Anne came prepared with typed notes which she handed to us.

"Here are some notes that will help answer a lot of questions you may still have, like; what to bring with you, what vaccines you need to get, what visas are required, etcetera. Speaking of which, you'll need to apply for American visas as soon as possible, for your return flight back home again."

"Thank you, this will be a great help," Denise replied.

"Well then, we better jump to it and start getting things sorted," I said to Denise.

"Give us a shout if you need help with anything," Mary-Anne added.

Finishing our beer, we thanked them for the opportunity and promised to stay in touch.

As we were leaving the yacht club, I looked over at Denise and said, " *Wow, this has really come as a unexpected surprise! Are you up for it?"*

"Absolutely, I think it could be a lot of fun!" she replied excitedly.

The following day, Denise and I rushed off to the American Embassy and applied for our visas.

In the interim whilst we waited to take receipt of the yacht for delivery, we were tutored in the basics of sailing. All the different nautical names of things on a boat was somewhat challenging to remember at first.

Charles was "old school" when it came to sailing. He also possessed a remarkable ability to read and forecast weather systems with extreme accuracy. With sixteen plus years of sailing experience as captain under his belt, we naturally trusted him implicitly and never doubted his capabilities.

Mary-Anne had been first officer for almost three years whilst doing yacht deliveries with Charles. It was clearly evident that she was well schooled by the master himself.

Two weeks later, we got a call saying that the yacht was ready for delivery. I was as excited as a five year old on Christmas day to see the yacht that we were going to spend a month on. It was a 40 foot "Leopard" sailing catamaran, specially built for a yacht charter company in the Caribbean. Wow, I felt like a multi-millionaire on board this incredibly beautiful boat!

While the boat builder was performing trials (which involved testing the boat), we were all feverishly busy purchasing groceries and all the other necessary supplies for the trip. This was a great learning experience for me – for example, I discovered what type and quantity of fresh vegetables, fruit, canned food, meat, poultry, emergency supplies, snacks, drinks, etcetera to take along. Then we all had to head off to the customs and immigration office to clear the boat out and have our passports stamped. The last stop was at the duty free store to purchase beer, liquor, cigars and many cartons of cigarettes – all which come in very handy when you need to barter trade for other things along the way.

All our friends and family gathered at the marina in Cape Town to wish us well for our exciting voyage to the Caribbean Islands. After a lot of hugs, kisses and teary eyes, it was time to cast off and set sail into the big blue yonder. This would be the last time that we would see land for the next ten or so days until we reached St Helena Island, which is located almost slap-bang in the middle of the Atlantic Ocean, between Brazil and North Africa.

Each of us had to stand watch at the helm on a two hour rotational basis. Responsibilities whilst standing watch included: keeping a look out for other vessels and lost shipping containers that had fallen off ships during rough seas, ensuring that we remained on course, logging our position on a paper chart in case the electronic navigation equipment failed and keeping a good look-out for fishing nets and long lines.

From the moment that we set sail in Cape Town, it was plainly obvious that Mary-Anne's demeanor had suddenly changed. All of a sudden, she became a super bitch on steroids, yelling at us and barking orders like an army sergeant.

One evening when she came to relieve my watch at the helm, she looked at the "Electronic Chart Plotter" and noticed that we had changed course. Without first enquiring why or who changed course, with a wild look in her eyes she yelled at me, "*You f***ing moron, who gave you f***ing permission to change course?*"

Before I could tell her that it was Charles that changed course, she screamed at me again, "*I'm the first officer on board this boat and I will make it f***ing hell for you and your wife if you don't obey my orders!*"

I was so taken back by her sudden outburst that I was lost for words. The only thought that came to mind was that this woman had lost her frigging marbles! Without saying a word, I turned around and retired to our cabin. Needless to say, the next morning I told Denise what had happened the previous evening. She confided with me that Mary-Anne had also become very bitchy towards her. We both decided that it was time for us to have a chat with Charles and sort matters out.

Over coffee that morning, Denise and I sat down with Charles and told him what had happened. From the look on his face, it was apparent that this wasn't the first time that crew had experienced problems with Mary-Anne. He assured us that he would have a chat with her and rectify the situation.

Two evenings later, when I came to relieve Mary-Anne from her watch, she went down to her cabin, only to return minutes later buck-naked other than a skimpy top. She squeezed herself onto the seat next to me at the helm and immediately started to grope my genitals. The more I pushed her hand away, the more aggressive she became. *"I want you to f**k me,"* she blurted out.

"Mary-Anne this isn't going to happen!" I said sternly, all the while pushing her away from me.

"You're going to regret this," she replied and returned to her cabin. Shortly afterwards I heard her screaming repeatedly on top of her voice, *"The mother f***er tried to rape me, the mother f***er tried to rape me!"*

Within seconds, Charles arrived on deck with Mary-Anne in tow behind him. It was then that I noticed that she had ripped the front of her top, thereby exposing her breasts. Before either of them could get a word out, I yelled, "*Charles, she is frigging lying! She tried to have sex with me and I refused. There is no way in hell that I'm going to have sex with a deranged psychopath! In fact, when we arrive at St Helena Island, Denise and I are getting of this frigging boat!*"

Thank God, the following day we arrived in St Helena Island. The time had finally arrived to get off this boat and away from this crazy woman. After dropping anchor, Charles came and pleaded with me to please stay. He went on to say that he could not complete the delivery without us and promised that he wiould sort Mary-Anne out.

"Let's stay for a couple of days and chill out. If you guys are still adamant about getting off the boat, then I'll understand. I desperately need your help, my friend, this will make or break my career as yacht delivery captain," he pleaded.

After a couple of days chilling out on the Island, Denise and I discussed our options. At the time, there wasn't an airport on the island. The only means to or from the Island was by a ship, which was only scheduled to arrive at the island in two weeks' time. On the other hand, we could continue the trip to Brazil, which would take ten days or so. If we then decided that enough was enough, we could easily find a flight back to South Africa. It would also be a lot easier for Charles to find replacement crew to complete the remainder of the trip to the Caribbean.

Denise and I got back on board and shared with Charles that we had decided to continue the trip to Brazil, only to save his hide. However, I also made it ultimately clear that we weren't going to tolerate Mary-Anne's bull sh*t any longer. He promised that he would keep her in check and that we wouldn't experience any further problems from Mary-Anne.

Midway into the trip to Brazil, things verbally erupted violently between Mary-Anne and Charles late one afternoon whilst Mary-Anne was on watch. Things got so loud and out of hand that I decided to go up onto the aft deck and see if everything was okay. During this time, Mary-Anne, (who was supposedly on watch), was sitting on a bunk near the back of the boat. I assumed position at the helm as there was no-one standing watch during this episode.

She was screaming on the top of her voice at Charles, "*I wish you'd die, you piece of sh*t!*" All the while, Charles tried to calm her down and defuse the situation. I noticed that she was still wearing her safety harness, to which a length of rope was tethered to the helm seat. This was a safety measure in case someone fell overboard.

The screaming and cursing continued for several more minutes. There was no doubt in my mind that Mary-Anne had completely lost it. After calling Charles every name under the sun, she eventually got up from the bunk and proceeded to undo her safety harness. Initially it appeared that she was going back inside the boat and the very next second, she took two big steps and jumped overboard. It looked as if everything was happening in slow motion. The fear in her eyes will be etched in my mind forever as she leapt into the ocean.

Instinctively, I hit the "M.O.B." (Man-Over-Board) button on the chart plotter; which placed a marker on the GPS indicating where she had jumped overboard. I heard Charles screaming behind me, "*Oh my God, oh my God, oh my God!*"

Charles was so bewildered and shook up, that I simply had to take control.

"Charles, take over the helm and start the engines, while I take the main sail down," I shouted to him.

We turned the boat around and started heading back towards the marker I placed on the GPS. Meanwhile, with all this commotion happening, Denise came up onto the aft deck. I instructed Charles to look out ahead of him, whilst Denise took up position on port (left) and I on starboard (right) side of the boat, scanning the ocean for any sign of life.

The odds were very low that we would ever find her again. Not only was it becoming dark very quickly, the ocean was also churned up with huge swells and white foam on the crests of the waves, making it impossible to see anyone in the water.

When we reached the marker, we turned the boat around and headed in the same direction we had been sailing when she jumped overboard.

As it became darker and darker, Charles kept on screaming, "*oh God, she's f***ing gone, she's f***ing gone!*"

This was a given, there was absolutely no way we'd ever see Mary-Anne again.

21

"Get your sh*t together Charles. Keep looking," I blurted out in sheer desperation, because I knew full well that this was the end.

This saga unwittingly triggered dark, bone chilling memories of a dreadful experience I had whilst scuba diving in Mozambique almost ten years ago...

3

Divers Lost at Sea

THERE IS AN AWESOME scuba diving resort at a little village called "Ponta do Ouro", which is remotely located on the southeast coast of Mozambique, bordering South Africa. My visit there was shortly after the civil war had ended. This meant that one had to adhere to strict safety procedures, one of which was NOT to stray off the main road leading to and from the border post and "Ponta do Ouro". This was due the fact that there were thousands of live landmines everywhere, which still had to be painstakingly recovered and defused by the military. In fact, whilst we were there, the lighthouse keeper was blown up by a landmine upon his return to the village from the lighthouse.

I had just obtained my "PADDI Dive Master" certification, which resulted in me leading dive groups on diving excursions in return for free dives for myself. In no time at all, I was racking-up hundreds of dives in my log book.

One day, unannounced the "Jacques Costau" oceanographic film crew rocked up at the resort. Their mission was to document on film how fish rid themselves of pesky parasites with the aid of sharks. Evidently, when a school of fish would swim behind a shark, fish would intermittently dash out from the school and brush up against the coarse flank of the shark – thus ridding themselves of parasites.

The ideal dive spot to film sharks was at a reef called the "Pinnacle", some twelve miles offshore. Not only was this home to an array of shark species, there were also huge numbers present at any given time.

Seeing the "Jacque Costau" dive team kit up in their silver neoprene wetsuits, with custom designed triplex-carbon-fiber scuba tanks and custom designed helmets with built-in flash lights, it looked like they had just walked off a "Star Wars" film set.

Due to the fact that I knew the reef intimately, I was honored and privileged to join the crew on their first dive at the "Pinnacle". I had to remain some five meters above the dive team, which comprised of a camera man flanked by a diver on either side armed with powerful underwater spot lights. There was a fourth diver just above them wielding a speared fish dangling just above the camera lens, in order to attract sharks with their mouths dramatically agape, dashing in and out of the frame of the camera.

It didn't take long for the sharks to begin a feeding frenzy, each trying to get a bite from the tasty morsel dangling tantalizingly from the end of the spear. Within mere seconds, the sharks were darting voraciously all around us with arched backs, cracking their tails so hard that it sounded like loud gun shots underwater.

I had never experienced anything as nerve wrecking and dramatic as this in my life before. The water looked as if was boiling, as dozens of sharks of every description milled around us. To crown it all, I didn't have anything to defend myself with other than a worthless little dive knife which was strapped to my leg. Whilst I was keeping an eye on a shark, jaws agape, shooting up below me, all I could think of doing was to pull my legs up and in the last millisecond, kick the shark on its' snout with all my might. As the shark got within a foot or so from my coiled legs, it suddenly veered away – only to be followed by another shark, approaching me at lightning speed from a different angle.

I was absolutely consumed with fear, so much so that I was convinced that within seconds we were going to be shredded alive by the multitude of sharks. Almost in a panic state of mind, all I could think of was to get out of the water as quickly as possible. Hardly had this sudden impulse crossed my mind, I realized that if I rose to the surface alone, I would easily be singled out as easy shark bait.

I prayed that the dive team would come to their senses and start surfacing. Not a chance, they weren't about to do anything of the sort with all the action-packed dramatic footage being captured on film.

After what felt like an eternity, the divers below me slowly started to make their way back to the surface. Needless to say, once we broke the surface, I was the first one back on board the safety of the dive boat. Never in my life had I ever felt so intimidated, helpless, petrified and scared sh*tless – to the extent that my legs felt like they had turned to jelly.

The following day, the weather turned out for the worst with thunderstorms, heavy rain, strong winds and dark clouds filling the sky. Late that afternoon, the "Jacques Costau" dive team saw a slight break in the weather and decided that there wasn't a moment to waste; they had to get back out there.

It was decided that the captain of the dive boat would take the dive team back out to the "Pinnacle" again and that he would join them on the dive, whilst I and one of the team's back-up crew would remain on the boat. Our job was to keep the engines running and follow the diving buoy to which a line was attached and reeled out by the divers as they descended into the big blue. This turned out to be a mammoth task, trying to keep an eye on the buoy in the choppy ocean. It was near impossible to remain abreast of the buoy bobbing up and down in the big, white foam-crested waves and strong winds. More importantly, we also had to watch for the dive team signaling us by yanking on the buoy. The signal meant that they were at their safety stop which was five meters below the surface, where they had to decompress in order to prevent them from getting the bends.

We had calculated that they had to reach their safety stop forty five minutes into their dive. Due to the fact that they had to decompress below the surface for an additional fifteen minutes of their dive time, they needed us to lower two dive cylinders down to their safety stop.

It was a daunting task straining our eyes on the bobbing buoy in the rough ocean. The swells were so big, that every time the buoy slid down the back of the swell, we'd lose sight of it. To complicate matters even more, their back-up crew member that remained on the boat with me was French and couldn't speak a word of English.

Every couple of minutes, I would check my watch to see when they would be approaching their safety stop. Forty five minutes came and went and there was still no signal from them. Knowing that the dive team members were hard core divers, I thought to myself that perhaps they were pushing the envelope to the limit.

Fifty minutes came and went, still no signal from the divers. With hand gestures, I signaled on my watch to the French crew member that their time was up, they HAD to be at their safety stop! Fifty five minutes went by without any signal from them. It was now a matter of life or certain death, they have to decompress at their safety stop. Due to the duration of their dive, they would surely be out of air by now as well.

After an agonizing hour with our eyes laser focused on the buoy, I decided to pull up next to the buoy and see if I get any response from the divers by tugging on the line from above.

With a boat hook in hand, my crew attempted several times to hook the line that was attached to the buoy to no avail. Out of shear frustration, I leaned over the boat and grabbed hold of the buoy only to realize that the line was no longer attached. *"Oh my God,"* I yelled, *"We've been following a dead buoy!"*

Still reeling from the previous days' near death experience, I was immediately consumed with sheer horror, realizing that we had lost the divers out at sea. It is difficult to express in words how dreadful it felt that I was responsible for the safety of the divers. Having said that, there was no hope in hell that we could have noticed that the line had become unattached from the buoy in that rough ocean.

Thoughts instantly raced through my mind, *"How long into the dive did the line become unattached? When did the divers realize that there was no longer a buoy at the end of the line? Did they make it to their safety stop with enough air to decompress? How far have we drifted from the dive site?"*

To add injury to insult, it was becoming dark very quickly which would make it near impossible to find the divers in the rough ocean. Not only that, there wasn't a GPS on board either. I had absolutely no idea where the dive site was located other than it being twelve miles off-shore. The dive boat captain made use of triangulated landmarks to locate the dive sites, which was why there wasn't a GPS on board.

Every minute that passed, the possibility of finding the divers diminished rapidly. In addition to that, the divers were easy pickings in the shark infested waters. There was no time to waste; I had to find them quickly! But, where?

I'm very fortunate that I have the ability to calm myself down and come up with a plan of action in a crisis. The first logical plan was to head back towards the direction from which we had drifted. With that said, we immediately started making headway into the oncoming choppy swells, which felt like being in a washing machine. We could only scan the surface of the ocean every few seconds, when the boat reached the crest of a wave. For the majority of the time, we were either going down the back of a wave or edging our way up onto the crest of the next wave.

I thought of calling for help but there wasn't a two-way radio on board. At the time, there weren't luxuries such as cell phones around either, especially out in the sticks in a third-world country.

Thirty five minutes had already passed without any sight of the divers. It was really starting to become dark quickly, so I had to come up with another plan of action. With hand gestures and pointing to my wrist watch, I tried conveying my plan of action with my fellow French crew member, "*We'll search for another five minutes and if we still hadn't found them, we'll make our way back to the shore and raise the alarm to get as many boats in the water to broaden our search.*"

Another five minutes went by when I decided that now was the time to head back to the shore. We had barely started making headway back to the shore, when I noticed a little black dot on the crest of a wave some hundred and fifty yards away. Taking a second look, that's when I saw a second and then a third dot on the crest. Almost in disbelief at what I'd seen, I immediately changed direction and headed towards the area where I saw the three dots. I kept thinking to myself, "*Please God, let it be the divers!*"

It was absolutely nerve wrecking trying to keep an eye on the dots bobbing up and down as the waves rolled in. One moment we could see them and the very next second they were gone again. It was impossible to take a head count due to the ocean being so choppy. All the while I was thinking to myself, "*I hope everyone is okay?*"

As we got closer, to my relief, I could see all five heads bobbing up and down over the foamy crests of the waves.

I don't know who was happier to see each other, them or us? Not that it mattered anyway because everyone started screaming with joy with huge smiles on our faces!

"*Thank God you guys are okay!*" I yelled out to them.

Once we got everyone safely back on board, we all embraced each other with tears in our eyes from sheer relief that everyone made it.

"*It's time to head back, boys, them ice cold frosties are waiting!*"

4

The Moment of Truth

"*WHAT ARE THE CHANCES* of experiencing someone lost out at sea for a second time?" I thought to myself. Any hope of ever seeing Mary-Anne again had dissipated from our minds. She had been in the water for at least forty five minutes already.

I thought quietly to myself, "Has she perhaps become so exhausted that she drowned?"

Just as the last of the sunlight rays skimmed the crest of the foamy waves, I saw a little head bob up on a swell, probably a hundred-plus yards away to starboard of the boat. This was a one in a billion chance of ever seeing her again.

In the split second that I saw her, thoughts raced through my mind, "F*ck this bitch, I didn't see her. This is the end of the misery she's put all of us through."

Hardly had these thoughts crossed my mind, when my conscience got the better of me and I shouted out to Charles, "I see her, I see her!"

Still in a state of disbelief, Charles replied, "What is it?"

I shouted back at him, "Charles it's her, turn the boat 45 degrees to starboard!"

I tried keeping my eyes on her but in vain, I couldn't see her, she was gone again. Now I was beginning to question what I had just seen, "Was it really a person that I saw on the crest of a wave a second ago?"

"Where is she, where the f*ck is she?" Charles kept repeating over and over again.

Straining my eyes in the cover of darkness, I had lost sight of her. She had completely disappeared from sight forever.

"Denise, bring me a flashlight," I shouted. Denise quickly returned with a flashlight and handed it to me. I kept scanning the foamy-crests of the waves as they rolled by, but there was no sign of her.

All the while, scenarios were milling through my mind, like, "To which authorities are we going to report this incident to? What are we going to tell them? Are they going to believe our story that she committed suicide or, did we bump her off ourselves in order to finally get rid of this psychopath?"

Charles shut the engines down in the last hope of maybe hearing her screams for help. Nothing, absolutely nothing! We had by then surrendered to the realization that she was gone, never to be found again.

"Do we broadcast a "Mayday" distress call on the radio?" I asked Charles.

"What will it help? She's gone!" he replied somberly.

"It doesn't matter Charles, do it anyway even if it is just to cover our asses to prove that we at least did something," I replied.

With shaking hands, Charles grabbed the mike and put out the distress call on channel 16 on the VHF radio, "May Day, May Day, May Day, this is....." he stopped midsentence. Due to the fact that it was a brand new boat, it hadn't been given a name yet.

"Just say sailboat," I quickly filled in.

With that, Charles completed the distress call which included our co-ordinates.

There was absolute silence on the radio. No one heard our distress call. No one said a word. Each in our own little world; thoughts milled through our minds of what had transpired that dreadful day. Even though she was a very, very sick person and an absolute bitch of the first waters, I still felt sorry for her that she had to end her life in such a terrifying and tragic way.

With the flashlight still in hand and scanning the ocean aimlessly in despair, I got up to go and pour us each a stiff drink to calm our nerves. As the beam of the flashlight fell towards the side of the boat, I saw her floating in the water, not even ten feet from the boat.

Quickly I yelled out to Denise, "Bring me the buoy!"

"Charles, start the engines quickly, she's here, she's here!" I screamed.

We came alongside and I threw the buoy out towards her. She refused to take hold of it. I yelled out to her, "If you think I'm going to jump into the ocean and rescue you, you are hugely mistaken. Now take hold of the f***ing buoy!" With that, she grabbed the buoy and we pulled her onboard.

I ordered Denise to take Mary-Anne below deck and let her have a nice hot shower. Whilst Denise was helping her into the shower, Mary-Anne repeatedly said, "Mommy don't leave me, mommy don't leave me."

After putting her to bed, I poured each of us a drink. We were all spent from the anxiety, terror and finally, relief. It was nothing other than a sheer miracle that we found her.

For the remaining five days of our trip to Brazil, we shared Mary-Anne's watch between the three of us. There was no way in hell that we were going to allow her to stand watch, considering the fact that she had suicidal tendencies. What if she decided to steer the boat directly in front of a big cargo ship and kill us all?

I've never been so glad to see land again. We moored the boat at a marina in Fortaleza and decided there and then that Mary-Anne had to get off the boat. Not only was she a risk to herself, she was an imminent danger to the rest of us as well.

Charles accompanied Mary-Anne to the airport to see her off. Due to the fact that she was so unpredictable, I personally think he went with her just to make damn sure that she did in fact board the plane back to South Africa.

Despite the tight delivery schedule, the three of us decided that we were just going to chill out for a couple days in Fortaleza, before setting sail for the final leg of our journey to St Maarten in the Caribbean.

Fortaleza, as is the rest of Brazil, is an extremely impoverished city. The beachfront is lined with beautiful hotels, restaurants and condos, commonly known as the "tourist strip". Barely two blocks behind, are the slums with drug-infested streets inhabited by the poor, unemployed and destitute. One thing that was very noticeable though, is that the Brazilian people are exceptionally friendly and appreciative of the little they have.

After two days of relaxation, we set sail again. For the first time on the trip, we experienced a relaxed and peaceful atmosphere on the boat – the way it was meant to be. Charles was also noticeably a lot less stressed and wound up. We played load music, danced, laughed, enjoyed sipping on late afternoon sundowners and, in general, just had an awesome time.

We were approximately three hundred miles north of Fortaleza, when Denise and I woke up one morning to a very strange and bizarre atmosphere. It was as if we were encapsulated in a cocoon of orange-brown colored haze all around us. The haze was so intense, that one couldn't see further than fifty yards around the boat.

"Charles, what's this haze?" I enquired.

"F*ck me if I know, I've never experienced anything like this before," he replied, with a concerned tone in his voice.

What amplified the situation was the fact that charter yachts aren't equipped with radars. This meant that we had to exercise extreme diligence looking out for other vessels camouflaged somewhere in the haze. We were constantly on edge, every second of the day!

Twenty four hours went by without the haze easing up one iota. It felt as if we were trapped on another planet somewhere in the universe. What made it even more confusing was that we were almost three hundred miles from land. So where and how did this haze come from?

We were imprisoned in the haze day and night, which just added to the feeling of absolute helplessness and despair. Unlike driving through heavy fog, where one can just pull off the road for a while and wait for it to pass, we simply had to endure this bizarre and terrifying phenomenon we found ourselves in.

At around noon on the third day, the haze eventually started to dissipate. It was only then that we noticed an orange tinge on the sails and deck. Upon further investigation, we discovered that this comprised of very fine, orange-brown colored dust. The question still hovered as to where did this come from?

Well, it so happened that Charles had brought a couple of "National Geographic" magazines with him. Whilst I was paging through one of the magazines, low and behold, there was an article about this phenomenon we had just experienced. It revealed that each year, over one hundred million tons of Saharan dust from the west coast of Africa, gets blown some three thousand miles across the Atlantic Ocean.

It was such a relief to finally be released from this cocoon we were held hostage in for the past three days! At long last we could see the open ocean, sun and stars again.

A couple of days later, we finally arrived at Oyster Pond in St Maarten where we delivered the boat to its new owners.

That evening, Denise and I went over to a little bar in the marina and ordered a nice bottle of red South African wine. I commented to the bartender that the bottle of wine is from the same region where we lived in South Africa. A guy sitting at the bar overheard me saying this, looked over to me and introduced himself. He said that he was also from South Africa and that he was crew on a yacht delivery a couple of weeks ago.

"Oh, really! My wife and I were also crew on a yacht delivery. We just arrived today."

"Who was the boat captain that you guys crewed with?" he enquired.

"Charles and Mary-Anne," I replied.

"Are you f**king kidding me? I was crew with them on the previous trip," he quickly added.

"I don't know how your trip went, but ours was an absolute nightmare!" I exclaimed.

"Let me guess, it was that bitch Mary-Anne. Right?"

After taking a sip of wine, I replied, "Oh, my gosh, her reputation certainly precedes her."

"Man, you won't believe what sh*t she did to me. She accused me of trying to rape her whilst I was standing watch one evening" he complained.

"You too! She did exactly the same thing to me!" I exclaimed loudly.

I went on to tell him the whole saga of her jumping off the boat in an attempt to commit suicide.

"Poor Charles was a wreck," I added.

"There's no doubt that she's a damn psychopath!" he concluded.

Well, that was the end of our first sailing experience. Besides the horrid nightmare with Mary-Anne, it was an incredibly awesome experience, far beyond our wildest dreams!

We thanked Charles for bringing us there safely and wished him well.

Two days later, Denise and I finally arrived home. As typical South Africans, we couldn't wait to invite our friends over, have a "braai" (BBQ) and share our "adventurous" sailing stories with them.

"Keep your face always toward the sunshine - and shadows will fall behind you."

Walt Whitman

5

Protected by Guardian Angels

AS IF IT WERE choreographed specifically for a Hollywood block-buster, I have to share this true story as it unfolded, whilst Denise and I were living in Tanzania, some ten years earlier.

Before I get ahead of myself again, I'll start where it all began, whilst exploring our dream of setting-up a scuba diving lodge in Mozambique.

Our next door neighbors "Wolf and Sue" shared the same passion for scuba diving as Denise and I did back in South Africa. Every opportunity that we got, we headed off to the coast for a couple days to go and blow some bubbles. It was on one of our scuba diving excursions in southern Mozambique that we decided to open a scuba diving lodge. The civil war had just ended and it was a great opportunity to set this up on the north-east coast of Mozambique.

With a business plan in hand, Wolf and I made an appointment with the Mozambique Government and excitedly shared our ideas with them. Now that the war was over, they were only too glad to see much needed investments coming into their country, so much so that they gave us carte blanche with any location or property we desired.

Eagerly, Wolf and I set off in his 4x4 truck to explore potential coastal regions along the north east coast of Mozambique. We identified a spot that looked rather promising on the map, called "Ponta da barra Falsa" and took off early the next morning to do some exploring.

Following our map, we exited the main road and headed east towards the coast, bumping along on a very sketchy road to begin with. The further we drove through very dense rural vegetation, the more dodgy the road became. We passed a couple of coconut-palm-leaf huts inhabited by a handful of indigenous locals, who joyfully waved their hands at the first two white guys they had seen in several years. One moment we were still driving on a pot-holed, hellish road and the next second, it had diminished to a mere two-wheel track.

After traversing very dense vegetation for over seven hours already, according to the map we should have been very close to the ocean. To the left of us were huge trees amidst the thick vegetation and to the right of us, lay very steep, thirty foot sand dunes. As we took a bend in the track, we were halted by a huge tree that had fallen right across the track. Initially we tried pulling the tree with a winch mounted on the front of the truck – to no avail. There was no way we could get around the tree, other than to go over it. Due to the girth of the tree being six foot in diameter, the plan was to pack branches on either side of the tree trunk. Since we didn't have the luxury of a chainsaw, we had to painfully sweat it out with a small, hand-held axe.

The sweltering humidity was absolutely unbearable, to the extent that we could only work five minutes at a time. An hour and a half later, we finally managed to maneuver the 4x4 over the tree trunk and continued on our expedition. We had barely travelled three hundred yards further, when we were welcomed by the most beautiful lagoon I had ever seen in my life.

Lost for words, Wolf and I just stood there in silence absorbing this awesome, pristine, natural splendor before our eyes. Coconut palm trees fringed the snow white sand banks on the left of the lagoon and to the right, the powder-blue ocean serenely lapped up on to the most beautiful beach you could ever imagine.

After standing there in awe for several minutes, we looked around us and saw this incredible little lodge tucked up on a little hillside overlooking the lagoon and ocean, a mere seventy yards away from us. Due to the overgrown vegetation around the lodge, it was obvious that it had been abandoned for some time already. Without a second thought, Wolf and I made our way up to the lodge and started scouting around the building, peering in all the windows. To our astonishment, the building and its' contents were still in pristine condition, as if the owners had hastily just left a couple of days ago on a walk-about.

There weren't any broken doors or windows. The beds and furniture were still in good condition, not to mention the impeccably well equipped kitchen, bar and lounge. This was an absolute no brainer– it would make for an ideal scuba diving lodge.

Still mesmerized by the treasure trove we had found, we heard a huge commotion developing near our vehicle. As we got closer, we were met by a group of locals shouting and waving their arms frantically at us. Seeing that neither Wolf nor I could speak any Portuguese, we were limited to communicating with the locals by means of rudimentary hand gestures.

Somewhat bewildered by the commotion, the locals didn't appear to be aggressive in any way, other than rambling off in Portuguese which we couldn't understand.

To our horror, it seemed from their hand gestures that the area was littered with deadly landmines, especially around the lodge. One of the elders shouted the word "*boom, boom, boom*" repeatedly and pointed towards a young boy missing one of his legs. It was obvious that he lost his leg as a result of a landmine.

In an instant, I got a cold chill running through my veins. I turned to Wolf and uttered the words, "W.*t.f. mate, we could have been killed up there!*"

The locals went on to gesture on our map, that the entire two-wheel track we had been driving on all this time was littered with live landmines. What we initially thought to be huge potholes in the road, was in fact evidence of previous landmine explosions.

Still in a state of absolute shock, I looked Wolf in the eye and uttered, "H*ow on earth did we manage to dodge all the landmines?*"

"*We're definitely not going back the way we came,*" Wolf sternly replied!

Due to the fact that the road was riddled with landmines and it was rapidly becoming late afternoon, we decided that we didn't have a minute to waste and make our way along the beach back to our base camp near "Maxixe", which was situated approximately some eight miles south of us.

To complicate matters further, we had to contend with an incoming tide which quickly narrowed the strip of beach between the ocean and the huge sand dunes on the other side of us. Once we committed ourselves to this route, there was no turning back! We simply had to persevere and ride this one out, come hell or (excuse the pun) high water...

After enduring some very harrowing moments along the way, we eventually made it safely back to base camp at early evening.

That night, beers in hand, Wolf and I sat around the fire and reminisced about our near death experience that day. There was no doubt in our minds that we were protected by "Guardian Angels" through it all.

It would take many years before this coastal region would be cleared from deadly landmines. As a result, Wolf and I decided to shelve our idea of setting-up a scuba diving lodge for the unforeseeable future and headed home the following day.

To this day, I still get goose-flesh every time I think about how close we were to death that day.

6

Drugs and Dubious Schemes

BARELY A WEEK LATER after Wolf and I returned to South Africa, we heard about a beach hotel in Tanzania which was available for lease. Leaving our wives at home, we immediately booked a flight the following day and took off to see what it was all about.

A driver picked us up at the airport and took us through to the hotel, which was approximately six miles north of the city, Dar es Salaam. We arrived at the hotel around nine thirty that evening and because we couldn't see much of the hotel at night, we checked into our rooms, keen for an early start the following morning.

Camera in hand, I was on the beach in front of the hotel, just as the sun rose above the ocean. My breath was taken away by the spectacular view before me. Less than half a mile from the beach was a small uninhabited island called Mbudya Island, with the clearest turquoise water surrounding it. I could see at least four shades of blue in the water as it lapped up onto the whiter-than-white powdery beach sand where I was standing.

I caught up with Wolf who was sitting at a little table on the beach enjoying his breakfast and freshly brewed coffee. I sat down next to him and poured myself a cup of this great aromatic java called "Africaf". It's probably the nicest coffee I've ever tasted in my life!

"Wow, I can certainly see myself waking up to this view every day of my life," I said to Wolf.

" Yip!" He replied.

" You can just imagine how good the diving must be with water so crystal clear," he indicated, whilst pointing out to the ocean.

After we had finished our coffee, we were taken on a tour through the somewhat derelict hotel. It clearly needed some serious remodeling and a fresh coat of paint throughout. There were 36 hotel rooms configured in a "U" shape to the north of the hotel, facing the ocean. To the south of the hotel was a large camp site which accommodated several tourist safari trucks. In-between the rooms and the camp site was the tiki bar and restaurant that overlooked the postcard picture scenery.

Though the hotel desperately needed a lot of work, the location was well worth the effort.

The following day, Wolf and I met with the State, who were the curators of the hotel, and concluded a very amicable ten year lease agreement.

We excitedly got onto the plane that afternoon and couldn't wait to share the great news with our spouses back home. The photos I had taken of the spectacular views ensured they didn't need much convincing.

Less than two months later, we had sold our houses, packed all our furniture and belongings into shipping containers, got our residence and work permits in order and took off to our new home in Tanzania.

When we arrived at the hotel, we hit the ground running, each with our respective responsibilities and chores. Wolf would take care of all the administrative requirements, Sue was in charge of housekeeping and front office, Denise took care of the restaurant and tiki bar, whilst I had to perform all the remodeling throughout the hotel.

In record time, we had local labor teams working feverously everywhere to get the hotel ready to accommodate our first guests. In conjunction with everything going on, I also started setting up our scuba diving center.

As the days went by, we were alarmed to see local fishermen using dynamite as a means of catching fish. Typically, they would approach the inner reef system by dhow (small wooden sailboat) and drop a couple sticks of dynamite tied together onto the reef. Seconds later, one could hear a load explosion followed by a tower of water shooting thirty-plus feet into the air. Using a hand-held net, they would then scoop up the dead and stunned fish in the water.

It got so bad, that we counted up to twenty blasts every day. Each blast would destroy approximately twelve square feet of reef at a time, resulting in over seven thousand square feet destroyed in a single month!

This was absolutely ludicrous! Besides the reefs that were being blown to smithereens, which would take many years to recover, the safety of scuba divers was also at stake. We urgently had to take action before somebody got seriously injured or killed.

We contacted the local police department, who in turn referred us to the marine police. They politely informed us that there wasn't anything they could do, due to the fact that they didn't have a boat to their disposal and therefore couldn't arrest the culprits. So that begs the question, "*Why on earth would they have a so-called marine police department, when they didn't even possess a boat to do their job?*"

One day, while I was busy working on the scuba diving center, a pick-up truck towing a brand new thirty foot catamaran power boat pulled up in our campsite. By virtue of the registration plate on the truck, I deduced that the two white guys in their mid-thirties were South Africans.

They introduced themselves as Ben and Pete and enquired whether they could stay over at our campsite for a couple of days. I welcomed them and helped them unhook their boat trailer.

A little while later, after they pitched their tents, they approached me with a briefcase in hand and asked whether I could secure their briefcase in a safe for them. Without me having to enquire what the briefcase contained, they opened it up and revealed packs and packs of U.S. Dollars. This immediately set off alarm bells in my head, "*W.t.f. were they doing travelling through Africa with so much cash on them?*"

Seeing the bewildered look on my face, they offered to explain themselves over a couple of beers at the tiki bar later that day.

The three of us sat around a table at the tiki bar, enjoying some ice-cold local beer called "Safari", when Pete, who was the more talkative of the two, started telling me how they landed up in Tanzania.

Ben, who owned the boat, had been fishing in Mozambique when he met Pete at the resort where they were staying. The fishing wasn't at all what he expected it to be and, to add insult to injury; he wasn't making enough money to cover the monthly installments for the boat.

In a place of sheer desperation, Ben was more than eager to hear Pete's scheme that would make them millions of dollars. Pete told Ben that he had contacts in Tanzania where he could buy large quantities of cocaine. The only problem was, of course, to get the drugs (especially in such large quantities) across the border, back into South Africa.

Now with Ben's help, they could get the drugs, load it onto the boat and follow the coast back to South Africa. That way they would avoid having to cross border posts and risking arrest. Once back home, they would split their takings equally between the two of them.

With nothing to lose, Ben accepted Pete's offer and the two of them took off for Tanzania.

After listening to their entertaining story, I agreed to them staying over, but made it ultimately clear that I wouldn't tolerate them dealing or keeping any drugs on our property. What they got up to outside our property was none of my business.

One evening a couple days later, whilst I was sitting at the tiki bar, Ben and Pete arrived and sat next to me.

Pete looked over at me and said, "*We've come to tell you that the deal is going down tomorrow. Because we trust you, we'll let you in on our plan.*"

"*What plan may that be?*" I replied.

"*Let me start by saying that the money in the briefcase isn't real, it's fake. Only the top notes of the packs are real, the rest is all fake. So, for that reason we've got to go about things a little differently.*"

Pete took another sip of his beer, briefly looked around him making sure nobody was within earshot, then leaned a little closer towards me and said, "*We're going to show them the money to prove that we in fact have the cash, but we're going to insist that we do the deal on the island, thereby avoiding the chance of a take-down by police.*"

I quickly chipped in, "*So, after taking the money, do you guys think they won't realize that the money is fake?*"

"*That's the reason why we're going to do the deal on the island. As soon as we hand them the money, we're going to shoot them, jump on the boat and take off, never to be seen again*" said Pete, with a slight grin.

"*Are you guys f***ing stupid! Dealing in drugs is one thing, murder is quite another.*"

By this time, I had already summed Pete up as to not being the brightest sparkplug around. That being said, I never imagined that he would entertain the idea of doing something really stupid like this.

Before either of them could get another word out, I continued, "*And another thing you morons haven't thought about, do you honestly think that they will come to the party unarmed? Crying out loud, mate, they're drug dealers – not Sunday school teachers!*"

With that, I got up from the table and left the two stooges sitting there.

Moments later, I returned with their briefcase, handed it back to them and growled, "*Here is your fake money. Come tomorrow, I want you guys to pack your sh*t and leave!*"

The following morning, I saw them jump into their truck and drive off, leaving all their stuff behind. I thought to myself, "*Perhaps they're just going to get some supplies from town and then leave.*"

They returned later that afternoon and asked me if they could stay one more night and then leave early the next morning. I said that was okay, as long as they didn't get up to any illegal activities on our property. They thanked me and took off in a taxi cab.

Later that evening, I noticed three shady characters wandering around the hotel and speaking to our staff. They hung around for a couple of minutes and left again. Being curious as hell, I approached one of the staff and asked what these guys wanted. The staff member said that they were looking for Ben and Pete, whereupon he replied that they weren't there and that's when they left.

"*What the hell did these two idiots get up to this time? Why are there people looking for them?*"

We didn't see them for the rest of the evening, nor the following morning. By noon there was still no sign of them anywhere. So I walked over to their tents in the campsite and peeked inside to see if their belongings were still there. Sure enough, everything was still as they left it. Besides, Ben's truck and boat was still there where he parked it.

By that evening, I became rather concerned as to what had happened to them. Thoughts started racing through my mind, "*What if they tried to pull a fast one on the drug dealers and got bumped off? However, if they were murdered, why were there people looking for them? Should I call the police and report them as missing persons?*"

But then again, I didn't want to get in the middle of things either.

The following day came and went and still there wasn't any sign of them. By now, everyone at the hotel got really worried that something had happened to them. Another possibility crossed my mind, "*What if they've been arrested and locked up somewhere?*"

So I called several police departments and enquired whether they've made any arrests of men following the description I gave them. Nothing, there was no record of any arrests made anywhere.

Three days had gone by without any sign of either of them. It's as if they had just vanished into thin air. I went over to their tents again to see if the briefcase was there. No sign of the briefcase either, which just added to the mystery of their disappearance.

Early morning on the fourth day while on my way to the campsite, I saw Ben sitting on the beach. He looked as if he hadn't taken a shower nor shaved in days. In fact, I remembered him wearing the same clothes, albeit a lot dirtier, which he had worn on the day they left in the taxi cab, four days previously.

"W.t.f. happened to you guys? Where did you disappear to? Where's Pete?" I fired off before he could reply to my first question.

Ben took a deep breath and said, *"Man it's a long story."*

In anticipation, I lit a cigarette and sat down next to him on the beach.

"So what happened, mate?" I urged him for an answer.

" We took a taxi into town to meet this guy at a casino, as we'd arranged earlier that day. We showed him the briefcase with the money and told him to bring a kilo of coke with him that evening, which he did. He opened the briefcase, took one of the bundles of cash and riffled through it with his thumb. Thank God the lighting was very dim in the casino or he would've immediately noticed that it was fake money. He placed the bundle of cash back into the briefcase, closed it and handed a sling-bag which contained a slab of coke over to Pete. Pete removed a pocket knife from his trousers and pierced a hole in the plastic wrap and retrieved a small sample of coke which he rubbed on his gums with his finger. Sure enough, it was legit. That's when we ordered a bottle of champagne to celebrate the

deal. *While this guy wasn't looking, Pete quickly squirted some tranquilizer into his drink, using a small syringe which he had in his hand."*

I quickly chipped in, *"Where did he get the tranquilizer from?"*

"He got it earlier that day from a vet."

"From a vet" I asked, surprised?

"Yip, he told the vet that he had a very ill donkey that he wanted to put down."

"Are you frigging kidding me? He could have killed this guy!" I blurted out!

Ben nodded sheepishly, knowing that it was a stupid idea.

"Before this dude could take a second sip, he was comatose. So we quickly propped him up in the corner of the couch where he was sitting, grabbed the briefcase, as well as the sling-bag, and took off before anyone noticed what had happened.

We jumped into a waiting taxi in front of the casino and headed for the airport.

Before I could ask another question, Ben continued with his story, *"Earlier that day, we bought two tickets to London. Whilst we were waiting to board the plane, I was absolutely freaking out in anticipation that this dudes' mates would be looking for us."*

"*But, what about the coke and the fake cash?*" I asked before Ben could get another word in

"*Security at the airport is very relaxed. Besides, if we had been caught, Pete was ready to bribe the officials – which was the norm in Africa, anyway.*"

"*But what about when you landed at the other end?*" I asked curiously, knowing that the authorities in the U.K. wouldn't take to this lightly...

"*Well that's just it. Whilst we were on the plane, Pete went to the bathroom and tucked the slab of coke into the front of his trousers. He then put a couple of magazines in the sling-bag just so that he didn't arrive there empty handed. When we landed at Heathrow airport, since we didn't have any luggage to retrieve, we headed straight to the immigration counter to have our passports stamped. Pete was ahead of me at the immigration counter, with me standing behind him, carrying the briefcase with the fake cash. The immigration official looked through his passport and that's when the questions started.*"

"*What is the purpose of your visit, sir?*"

"*Business,*" Pete replied.

"*How come you only have a one-way ticket?*" the official asked sternly.

"*We didn't know how long it would take to conduct business matters, so for that reason I don't have a return ticket as yet.*"

"Who is 'WE', sir?" the official quickly snapped back at Pete.

" That's when Pete turned around and pointed towards me. "

"Please step forward, sir?" the official beckoned to me with his finger.

"He flipped through my passport several times, taking note of all the stamps in my passport. "

"Please wait here. I'll be back in just a moment. " With that the official walked off with our passports in hand.

"I was sweating bullets by this time. He later returned with another official, who then asked us to accompany him. I knew then and there that we were in deep sh*t!"

"So what happened?" I urged.

" The official told me to take a seat outside an office and escorted Pete inside. Because I didn't want to be caught with the fake dollar bills, it was then that I decided that I had to come up with a plan quickly. I got up from my seat and quickly made my way to the public bathrooms, where I flushed the fake money down the toilet as fast as I could. Within minutes, I was seated back outside the office. The official peered out the door and waved me into the office. I have never been so scared in my life before. "

As Ben relived his nerve wrecking experience, I could see pearls of sweat forming on his forehead.

"The guy looked through both our passports again, looked up at us and said that they were going to deny us entry into the U.K. and that they were going to deport us on the next available flight back to Tanzania. He told us to wait in the office, while he got the deportation documents filed. I was so relieved that they didn't pursue matters further, other than deporting us."

He wiped the sweat from his forehead with his finger and continued with his story, *"The guy came back with the deportation documents in hand and informed us that we were scheduled on the first flight back to Tanzania, at ten p.m. the following evening. He also told us that under no circumstances were we allowed to leave the airport building. We agreed, shook his hand and left the office."*

"As soon as we got out of the office, Pete turned to me and said that he wasn't going to get on the plane. He said that he came to the U.K. to make some serious money and that he was sticking to his plan. I told him that he was frigging crazy and that I didn't want any part of this. It was then that I told him that I flushed the fake money down the toilet. He absolutely flipped and started cussing me for doing such a stupid thing."

"So did he actually stay behind?" I asked, wanting to get confirmation that he really did stay in the UK.

"Yip, he just simply walked out of the airport, without looking back."

"What a dumb ass! So, tell me, Ben, how did you get so dirty?"

"*I didn't have a penny to my name, so when I landed at the airport, I had to walk in the dark all the way back to the hotel. Needless to say, I tripped and fell several times along the way.*"

Sure, Ben did some really stupid things and I think probably more so, due to Pete's bad influence. I got up and said, "*I think you can do with a hearty breakfast and some of that good Java, mate.*"

"I dwell in possibility."

Emily Dickinson

7

Dynamite and Machetes

IN THE DAYS WHICH followed, Ben was rather helpful around the hotel with all the various remodeling projects going on. It was a win-win situation, whereby he would provide help wherever needed and, in return, we'd provide him with free board and lodging.

The more I got to know Ben, the more I saw a very desperate and broken man inside. Besides his dire financial situation, he missed his wife and six year old son terribly. They were still living in South Africa.

Due to the fact that Ben urgently needed the capital to pay off his boat and us needing a boat for our scuba diving operation, we agreed to settle the balance owing on the boat and give him five thousand dollars in cash on top of the deal.

At long last, we could go scuba diving and explore the reefs nearby. On one occasion, while we were out there scuba diving, a gang of ruthless local fisherman dropped dynamite not even seventy yards from where we were diving. The blast was so loud and powerful, that we all suffered ear and lung injuries.

Now that we had a boat, we were in a position to assist the marine police by taking them out on daily patrols to combat the rampant illegal and dangerous dynamite-fishing practices. This proved to be very successful, resulting in numerous arrests being made and large quantities of dynamite being seized.

As the remodeling of the hotel rooms neared completion, we decided to free up the hotel rooms that management was occupying and rent a house nearby. That was when we learnt of a house which was conveniently located some two hundred yards up the road from the hotel. It was owned by a corrupt government official, who also had several other properties throughout Tanzania. Due to the house standing vacant for some time already, he was only too pleased to rent his house to us for a mere twelve hundred dollars a month. The huge, double-story house comprised four bedrooms, three bathrooms, lounge, kitchen and dining room downstairs, with the upper-level mirroring the floor plan downstairs. This ideally suited our needs, in that management would occupy the upper lever and our family and friends could have the entire ground floor to themselves, whenever they came over to visit us.

Soon after we moved into the house, management decided that we would surprise Ben and fly his wife and son up to Tanzania. One evening, while we were all sitting in the restaurant, Ben's wife and son walked into the restaurant unannounced. Ben almost fell off his chair when he looked up and saw his wife and son standing in front of him. It was an awesome and very emotional moment that brought tears to everyone's eyes.

Ben's wife, Sheryl, was a very pretty gal in her mid-thirties, with shoulder length ginger hair and emerald-green eyes. His son, David, looked just like his father; a stocky little fellow, with crew-cut blonde hair.

Later that evening, we all retired to the house up the road from the hotel. Ben, Sheryl and their son David occupied the ground floor, and the rest of us went upstairs. Wolf and Sue's bedroom, located near the stairwell connecting the lower and upper levels, had a beautiful private little lounge on-suite. To the far end of the upper level, Denise and I had a nice bedroom with an outdoor balcony attached.

I had just sunken into a deep sleep, when we were rudely awakened by a very loud commotion going on downstairs, with lots of shouting and terrifying screaming taking place. The next moment, we heard a loud bang – what sounded like a shotgun went off inside the house. More bone-chilling screaming ensued. My immediate thought was that our house was being invaded and that they had just murdered Ben downstairs.

Since we weren't permitted to own any firearms, there was no way we could defend ourselves against the onslaught of cold-blooded murderers. Our only option was to hide. Thoughts raced through my mind that if they found us, they were certainly going to kill us. Hiding was definitely not an option!

I grabbed Denise by the hand and hastily made our way out onto the balcony adjoining our bedroom. As I peered over the balcony, I saw at least a dozen locals in front of the house, shouting loudly in Swahili whilst wielding machete's and sticks aggressively in the air.

Turning to Denise, I said, "*We've got to get out of here, they're going to kill us all!*"

With that, I climbed over the railing onto a twelve inch-wide ledge and started shuffling precariously along the ledge towards the back of the house, with Denise following closely behind me. My heart was pounding loudly in my ears as we stood motionless, with our backs propped-up against the wall.

The shouting continued for several more minutes, followed by two more shotgun blasts.

"*This is it*" I thought to myself, "*They've just murdered Sheryl and David as well!*"

"*We're going to die, we're going to die,*" Denise quietly sobbed next to me.

All of a sudden, things became eerily quiet. Were they now creeping around inside the house searching for Denise and I?

Gripped by absolute fear, we stood motionless for several more minutes without hearing another sound.

I turned my head towards Denise and whispered into her ear, "*I think they've left. I'm going to go check if it's safe to come down from here.*"

In order for me to get back inside the house, I had to gingerly slide across the front of Denise on this very narrow little ledge and return back the way we came.

Still not sure if they had in fact left, I cautiously peered around the corner of the balcony and made my way slowly into the house. The quietness was deafening!

When I reached the top of the stairwell, I could barely see the bottom of the staircase through the white-greyish smoke that had a sweet-gun-powder smell to it.

As I got to the bottom of the staircase, I noticed that the front door had been blown off its' hinges.

" *W.t.f. happened here?*" I thought to myself.

Looking down the passage to my left, I saw Ben lying motionless on the floor just outside their bedroom door. It was an absolutely horrific sight to witness; blood spattered on the ceiling, down the walls and pooling around his head. There was no doubt in my mind that Ben was dead.

I ran over to where Ben was lying motionless on the floor and knelt down.

Looking into his glazed, non-responsive eyes, I grabbed hold of his shoulders and screamed, "*Ben... hey Ben, can you hear me?*"

Just then, his wife came running out of their bedroom, carrying their son in her arms.

I was somewhat bewildered at first when I noticed her, due to the fact that I had heard three distinctive shotgun shots going off. I genuinely thought that they had all been killed.

"*Is your son okay?*" I shouted at her.

"*Good Lord, YES!*" she cried back.

"*You need to go back inside the room, don't let David see his father like this,*" I ordered.

Sheryl had hardly turned around when Sue and Wolf came flying down the stairs and down the passage to where Ben was lying.

"*Oh my God, is Ben dead?*" Sue shouted across to me as she saw Ben's motionless body and huge amounts of blood everywhere.

Without answering her, I kept shaking Ben's shoulders whilst shouting, "*Hey mate, can you hear me?*"

"*Are Sheryl and the kid okay?*" Wolf enquired.

"*Yes, they're fine,*" I replied.

My eyes scanned Ben's body to see where he had been shot. Other than blood spatter down the front of his white T-shirt, I couldn't see anything that resembled a gunshot. That's when I examined his head further, where it lay in a pool of blood. On the crown of his head, I couldn't help but notice a huge gaping gash, oozing with blood.

I looked up at Sue who was standing there and said, "*Sue quickly get me some towels!*"

Just then I heard Ben make murmuring and groaning sounds.

"*Be still, mate, we've got you. You're gonna be okay!*" I reassured him, whilst squeezing his hand.

Moments later, Sue returned with some towels. I clasped my hands on either side of his head, lifted it up and ordered Sue to wrap a towel around his head.

"*What can I do?*" Wolf enquired.

That's when I remembered that Denise was still outside standing on the narrow concrete ledge.

"*Please go outside around the back of the house and help Denise down from the ledge.*"

Without hesitation, Wolf took off running out the house.

"*Sue, help me turn Ben over onto his side, so that he can breathe,*" I ordered.

As we turned Ben onto his side, I saw another deep gaping gash across his upper back.

69

"Hand me another towel, please!" I blurted out, pointing to a heap of towels next to Sue.

Folding the towel into a square, I placed it over the wound.

"Keep pressure with your hands on the wound, I'm going to get something that we can place under him so that we can carry him to the truck."

I left Sue with Ben and went into a spare bedroom and retrieved a blanket from one of the beds.

In the interim, Wolf found a ladder near the side of the house and helped Denise down from the ledge.

Placing the blanket on the floor next to Ben, with Sue's help, we rolled Ben onto the blanket. Just then Wolf and Denise returned.

When Denise saw all the blood everywhere, she cried out, *"Is Ben okay?"*

"He's badly hurt; we've got to get him to a hospital as quick as we can!"

There was no sense calling for an ambulance. By the time they eventually arrived, Ben would have kicked the bucket long ago.

As if they had been ordered, two "askari's" (security officers) from the hotel appeared.

Due to Ben being a tall well-built guy, I knew that we were going to battle to get him into the back seat of the truck. The only option was to place a mattress in the back of the open truck and lay him on top.

With the help of the askari's, we each grabbed a corner of the blanket and carried him outside. Wolf quickly returned dragging a mattress behind him. In a jiffy, we had the mattress, with Ben lying on his side, in the back of the truck.

"Denise, quickly go inside and fetch Sheryl and the boy so that they can go with to hospital" I ordered.

Sheryl and her son jumped in the front, with Wolf driving, whilst I sat on the back of the truck and looked after Ben.

Sue and Denise remained behind at the house with the askari's watching over them. Denise had already calmed down a bit and had the sense of mind to call the police. Not that they were going to be of much help, seeing that they had to first find a taxi to convey them to the house. That's the kind of stuff one has to put up with when living in a third-world country.

Ben made murmuring sounds all the way to the hospital. I was thinking to myself that at least this was a good sign, even though he couldn't talk.

After what felt like an eternity, we finally arrived at the hospital, with Wolf honking the horn as we neared the front door.

Nursing staff came rushing out of the door to see what all the noise was about, not thinking of bringing a stretcher with them.

71

"Quick, bring a stretcher!" I barked at a nurse.

" What happened?" one of the nurses enquired.

"He was savagely attacked and has big lacerations on his head and back. He's lost a lot of blood!" I replied.

The nurse returned moments later, wheeling a stretcher in front of her. We hurriedly got Ben onto the stretcher and into the hospital.

"Get the doctor," I overheard one of the nurses say to another.

Within minutes, the nurse returned with the doctor in tow. He ordered all of us out of the E.R. and pulled the curtain closed behind him.

Still in a state of shock, Sheryl who was still cradling her son in her arms yelled, *"Is Ben going to die?"*

I placed my arm around her shoulders and gave her a hug. *"He's going to be fine. He's just lost a lot of blood,"* I said in an attempt to reassure her.

We all sat down on a bench outside the E.R. and I turned to Sheryl and asked, *"So, tell me what happened?"*

"Ben and I were sleeping, when we were awakened by a very loud bang inside the house. The next moment, a gang of black guys stormed into our bedroom and struck Ben on the head with a machete. Ben desperately tried to fight them off, but there were too many of them. They pulled him out of the bed

and that's when one of them slashed him across his back with a machete. I screamed at them not to hurt him, but they just continued to kick and punch him everywhere on his body."

Sheryl started sobbing loudly. *"I've never been so scared in my life,"* she cried holding her hands over her face.

I could just imagine how petrified she must have been, especially due to the fact that she just got off the plane in a foreign country, only a couple hours ago.

I placed my arm around her shoulders again and reassured her that everything was okay now.

Sheryl continued, as she relived the nightmare, *"I couldn't understand what they were shouting because they were speaking in another African language. I just kept on pleading with them not to kill Ben as they continued to kick him, while he was lying in the passage just outside our bedroom."*

"That's when I heard David crying in the next room. So I ran through the interleading doorway between the two rooms and put my arms around him. Shortly afterwards, the voices disappeared down the passage and that's when I heard two more loud shots go off inside the house. I knew in my mind that they had shot Ben. I was too scared to look out the door and remained there until you arrived."

Some time later, the doctor came out of the E.R. with a clipboard in his hands.

"How is my husband?" Sheryl pleaded with the doctor.

"He's doing okay now. We've sedated and intubated him, because he had great difficulty breathing on his own. We've also got some plasma drips going in the meantime, until we get drips with his same blood-type from the blood bank. The lacerations were very deep, but miraculously no vital organs were damaged. X-rays were taken and it shows that he has two fractured ribs on his left and another four on the other side. He's also no doubt suffered severe concussion resulting from the trauma to his head. Other than that, I think he will do just fine!" the doctor concluded.

"Can I see my husband now?"

"In just a moment, ma'am. They're going to transfer him to the I.C.U. and then they'll come for you. Just remember that he is in an induced coma and therefore won't be able to talk to you."

Sheryl thanked the doctor as he turned and walked off again.

"My nerves are shot guys, I'm going outside for a much needed smoke," I blurted out, while grabbing a packet of cigarettes from my trouser pocket.

With my fingers and hands still covered in dry blood, I lit a cigarette and inhaled deeply.

"What a f***ing night!" I thought to myself, exhaling slowly.

Wolf joined me outside, just as the sun was starting to rise.

"Who were these thugs?" he enquired.

Taking another drag from the cigarette, I looked over at Wolf and replied, "*Those were no gunshots we heard. These f***kers threw dynamite in the house. Did you see what the front door looked like?*" I enquired.

"*I think you're right mate. The moment I got that distinctive, lingering, sweet nitroglycerin whiff, I knew that was dynamite,*" Wolf answered.

"*Yip, this means one thing for certain. These cowards are dynamite fishermen,*" I growled back at Wolf.

"*Now we're going to fight fire with fire! They've got another thing coming if they think they will get rid of us by intimidating us. Besides, I'm really pissed off about what they did to Ben. He didn't deserve what they did to him.*"

The more I thought about it, the guiltier I felt, "*They got hold of the wrong guy – I was their intended target!*" I said angrily to Wolf.

"*I'm the one who took the marine police on patrols. I'm the one who was responsible for a lot of them being arrested and their stuff confiscated.*"

Wolf quickly chipped in, "*It's not your fault, mate. Remember when we all suffered ear and lung injuries due to them dynamite-fishing near us, while we were diving? These guys are ruthless criminals who don't give a sh*t!*"

"As sure as hell, I'm going to make it my life's mission to make these bastards pay for what they've done to us, watch this space!" I said sternly to Wolf.

8

Ex-wives and Bikers

ABOUT A WEEK LATER, Ben had recovered remarkably well from his attack, albeit still very tender as a result from having several fractured ribs. The doctor said that he was well enough to be discharged from hospital, but had to take it easy for a while.

In the interim, we decided that it was too risky for us to remain at the house, so we moved back to the hotel, where we at least had askari's on duty twenty four hours a day.

Sue was like a typical mother-hen over Ben. She would pop in to check on Ben several times throughout the day, fluffing his pillows and making sure he was eating properly and had enough fluids to drink. She even offered to look after young David in order for Sheryl to take some time-out and go scuba diving with us.

David appeared to be a real mommy's boy, always clinging to his mother and throwing little tantrums if he couldn't have his way with something or the other. Sheryl reacted by babying and pampering him until he got what he wanted. Not even five minutes would go by without him wining and crying again. I could see that this was p*ssing Ben off immensely.

Noticing that there was a lot of tension between Sheryl and Ben, we suggested that they take some time out and go over to Zanzibar Island for a couple of days. After all, they had both been under a tremendous amount of stress lately.

Zanzibar was a mere hour by ferry across from the hotel. We booked a very nice chalet for four nights on the beach for them. The setting is really tranquil and relaxing, with the beautiful powder-blue ocean right on their doorstep, snow-white beach sand, palm trees with hammocks stretched between them and cocktail drinks at a snap of a finger. They even had a play center with nannies to take care of the youngsters, so that mom and dad could just take some time out and relax.

It was barely two days later, when Ben arrived back at the hotel without Sheryl and David. He said that he couldn't take it any longer, with David being absolutely miserable twenty four hours a day. What really got to him was the fact that Sheryl wouldn't listen to him and stop pampering the child like a little girl.

Sheryl and David returned two days later, requesting that they sleep in a separate room from Ben. It was clear that there was still a lot of animosity between Ben and Sheryl. Perhaps a couple of days apart from each other would help the dust to settle and do them both good in order for them to discuss things rationally.

Being an early riser, I got up at around four-thirty one morning and noticed Sue leaving Ben's room with her sandals in her hands. It certainly looked very promiscuous and not being willing to say anything, I left it at that.

I wasn't sure if anyone else had also been noticing that Ben and Sue were spending more and more time in each other's company. Each time we would go scuba diving, the two of them would remain behind with an excuse that they had "chores" to do.

It was on one such occasion that we all went to Zanzibar for a two-tank dive, leaving Ben and Sue behind at the hotel. Some four hours later, upon arriving back at the hotel, the staff informed us that Ben and Sue, each carrying two suitcases, jumped into a taxi and took off together.

When Wolf arrived back at their room to take a shower, he noticed a "Dear Johnny" letter on the dressing-room table. In brief it said that Sue and Ben were in love with each other and that they were going to separate from their respective spouses.

Wolf wasn't one for showing his emotions, so as a result it appeared that he wasn't that upset with the whole saga. In fact, it was rather ironic because Wolf would often say, "*You can take my wife and bicycle, but you leave my beer and food alone!*"

I personally think that the demise of Wolf and Sue's relationship came about because Sue's maternal clock was ticking and Wolf wasn't interested in having any children.

It didn't appear that Sheryl was too upset about the break-up either. As if "quid pro quo" was the order of the day, Wolf and Sheryl also started having a fling with each other. It was certainly evident that it was merely sexual, rather than an actual romantic affair going on between them.

As the days became weeks, everyone was going about their daily tasks around the hotel as usual. In the interim, Ben and Sue had returned to South Africa and filed for divorce from their respective spouses. The divorce settlements were very amicable both ways, which resulted in speedy divorces being granted soon afterwards.

Whilst I was busy servicing the scuba diving boat engines one afternoon, a guy in his late thirties, with long blond hair, pulled up at the camp-site on a motorcycle. He introduced himself to me as Stefan and said that he had been touring through Zimbabwe, Zambia, Malawi and Tanzania on his bike. He continued by saying that he was from Germany and decided to take a year-long sabbatical to do some travelling through Africa.

It may appear to some, while surfing the internet, that touring through Africa would be a very cool thing to do. The reality, on the other hand, is that it's not as glamorous as it appears to be. Everything in Africa is a mission – especially if you are a foreigner. Authorities would often harass people for hours at border posts in order for them to solicit bribes. Things like, "*You don't have the right visas, or your yellow fever vaccination is out of date, or your vehicle doesn't have the correct paperwork, etc.*" weren't uncommon scenarios. If it isn't immigration intimidating you, then customs would be on the prowl for an easy buck or two. No sooner had you thought that you were through this ordeal, and then police would stop you at make-shift road blocks, soliciting more bribes from you. In short, it would become exceptionally tiring – not to mention, very expensive.

Stan, as he would be called later, was worn out from all the harassment and needed some time out. He offered to help out with maintenance chores around the hotel in exchange for a bed to sleep in and a plate of food on the table. It turned out that Stan was an exceptionally good mechanic, which earned him extra perks, such as a couple free beers after work.

Stan had a very attractive and pleasant demeanor about him. He always had a smile on his face and often had us in fits of laughter when sharing his experiences through Africa. Needless to say, the aura that he radiated, combined with his good looks, certainly caught the ladies' attention.

It wasn't long before Stan and Sheryl hooked up. Not only did he show a lot of affection towards Sheryl, he also developed a very nurturing and caring bond with David. It was as if David had somehow miraculously evolved into a very happy and cheerful young boy overnight. There was no doubt that a very loving relationship between Stan, Sheryl and David had soon developed.

The time was nearing for Stan to fly back to Germany which complicated matters between them. Stan had his own successful business as an auto-mechanic back home, yet on the other hand, Sheryl who grew up as an orphan in South Africa, didn't have any real reason for her and David to return to South Africa.

Out of the blue, a couple of days later, whilst we were all sitting around a table in the restaurant, Stan got down on one knee and asked Sheryl for her hand in marriage. With tears streaming down Sheryl's cheeks, she said yes. Stan removed a small brass ring which he made in the workshop from his trouser pocket.

"To make things official, this will have to do for now" and placed the ring on her finger.

Stan looked into Sheryl's eyes and said, *"I promise you when we get to Germany, I'm going to give you the biggest diamond ring you have ever seen."*

They kissed and embraced each other lovingly whilst we all clapped and wished them well.

"So, what's the plan Stan?" I jokingly enquired.

"Now that we are officially engaged, as my fiancé Sheryl and David can obtain the necessary visa's to return back to Germany with me."

We barely stood up from the table when a policeman arrived and requested to speak to me. I greeted him and asked what I could do for him?

"We received information that you are destroying our currency," he replied.

For a moment I was absolutely dumbfounded by his accusation. My immediate thoughts were that this just another cock-and-bull story, which inevitably was leading up to a bribe again.

" What are you talking about?" I enquired.

"The info that we received is that you drilled holes into twenty shilling coins and used them as washers. This is a very serious matter which carries lengthy jail sentences," he said sternly.

That's when it hit me like a sledgehammer. Due to us being so close to the ocean, everything rusted before your eyes. As a result, I used twenty shilling coins, which were nickel-clad-steel, as washers on an outdoor timber staircase. Besides, it would have cost a hundred shillings for one stainless steel washer of the same size.

"That is absolutely ludicrous, I would never do such a thing," I fired back at him.

"Shall we go see?" he replied, more as a command than a question.

Without skipping a beat, I replied angrily, *"I'm deeply shocked by such an accusation. Even if it were true, do you have a search warrant?"*

"No sir," he replied solemnly.

"Then I suggest you get your facts straight first. Once you do, then and only then do you return with a search warrant in hand. Now leave my property before I lay a charge against you for deformation of character and have YOU thrown in jail," I growled at him!

He spun around on his heels and left. From the look on his face, I could see that he was determined to return with a search warrant the following day and arrest me.

I was so close to having my ass being thrown in jail that I just stood there for several minutes reeling from absolute shock.

"I've got to do something quick before he returns with a search warrant in hand," I thought to myself.

I immediately rounded up Wolf, Stan, Denise and Sheryl for an urgent meeting.

I told them what had happened and said, *"After the staff leaves, at midnight, we'll have to remove every damn washer from that staircase and replace it with ordinary washers."*

"How many are there?" they enquired.

"Hundreds..."

Low and behold, we all worked feverishly throughout the night and replaced every single washer. Making sure that there wasn't a shred of evidence around, Wolf and I jumped onto our boat before the sun rose that morning and dumped the "washers" out in the ocean.

The policeman didn't ever return to the hotel again.

"Nothing is impossible; the word itself says 'I'm possible'!"

Audrey Hepburn

9

Crackdowns and Covert Operations

ONE AFTERNOON, THREE elders from a fishing village near us came over to meet with management. With the help of one of our staff members translating for us, we listened to what the elders had to say.

Sitting at a table outside, the elders began communicating with us. Referring to the attack on us, they began by saying that they were very sorry for what had happened. They were very appreciative for us being so brave in attempting to put an end to the illegal dynamite-fishing practices. They assured us that the majority of the village disapproved of the dynamite-fishing practices, because the fish numbers have dwindled exponentially as a result.

After a long pause, they dropped a bombshell. They said that this wasn't going to end because the marine police were involved.

I looked across at the others and said, " *Why aren't I surprised? It's Africa, what do you expect?"*

"How are they involved?" I enquired from the elders.

They elders replied by saying that it was in fact the marine police who were supplying the fishermen with explosives. Every day, when the thugs returned to the villages with their dhows filled with fish, the marine police were there, ready and waiting to receive their cut from the sale of fish.

I looked over at the translator and said, *"Please tell the elders that we aren't going to throw in the towel. We're going to fight this fight with everything that we've got, until the very end. And that's a promise!"*

The elders stood up, thanked us again and took off.

"So what are we going to do? How are we possibly going to fight this war against the dynamite fishermen, if the marine police themselves are involved?" Denise questioned, throwing her hands up in the air in despair.

"I'm going to write a letter to President Mkapa," I replied.

"*Do you genuinely think that President Mkapa is going to do anything about this?*" Denise asked.

"*Hey, we have nothing to lose. I'm going to give him an ultimatum which he cannot refuse.*"

Before anyone could get a word in, I continued, "*I'm going to tell him that we have several lobbyists across the world, who are at the ready to protest against tourism to Tanzania. If he doesn't react quickly, we'll mobilize protests across the globe and that the country will suffer dearly due to tourists not coming anymore. After all, tourists don't want to run the risk of being blown up, right?*"

"*You've certainly got a point there, Mac. But how are you intending to rally protests globally?*" Wolf asked enquiringly.

"*It's all smoke and mirrors, mate. He doesn't know if we indeed have lobbyists in place or not. The risk is way too high for him to gamble on this one,*" I replied reassuringly.

I wrote a very lengthy letter, detailing several facts, such as, "*How much capital investors such as ourselves have plowed into the country already, how many people we have created employment for and the families they feed, how much income the country stands to lose from tourism annually, thousands upon thousands of businesses will close and an even greater number of people will be out of jobs, etc.*"

I didn't want to be overly optimistic, but it doesn't take a rocket scientist to figure this one out! As they say in Africa, *"Anything is possible!"*

In the interim, with the help of the locals, we formed and registered an N.G.O. called M.A.C.T. (Marine Action and Conservation of Tanzania) with the mission of protecting the ocean and its reefs. Only once we did that, did we learn how widespread the issue with dynamite-fishing was. Not only was it as far north as Kenya and all the way down south, including Mozambique; islands off the coast of Tanzania, such as Pemba, Zanzibar and Mafia, were also heavily plagued with this destructive fishing practice for many years.

The W.W.F. (World Wildlife Fund) who had been trying to combat this problem for several years on Mafia and Zanzibar islands without any success, let us know, in no uncertain terms, that we didn't stand a snowball's hope in hell of ever making headway with this problem.

"That remains to be seen," was my response to them.

Probably about a month later, I was abruptly woken up very early one morning by loud banging on our door. When I peered out the door, one of our askari's said to me, *"Mister Mac you must come quickly, the army is here!"*

"W.t.f. is going on this time?" I thought to myself.

"Fuggit, there's never a dull moment in Africa, is there?" I said to Denise, who was rather bewildered by all the commotion.

I quickly got dressed, threw on my flip-flops, put my cigarettes in my pocket and took off out the door.

As I rounded the corner to the parking lot, there were military vehicles and army personnel as far as the eye could see.

An army officer walked up and introduced himself to me. He said that they were conducting a national crackdown on illegal dynamite-fishing practices, under direct order of the President. He continued by saying that the army as well as the navy would be working jointly in this operation.

I mused, *"This is a criminal matter, so why is the military involved? But then again, anything is possible in Africa."*

I was absolutely delighted, knowing that the letter I wrote to the President resulted in this massive operation and that something was finally being done about this.

I shook his hand and asked him to personally thank the President on our behalf.

At breakfast that morning, I couldn't wait to share the good news with everyone. Finally there was light at the end of the tunnel.

We went about our business as usual that day, noticing later that afternoon that a navy frigate had dropped anchor opposite our hotel. I called Denise over and asked her to quickly bring me my binoculars. When I focused on the flags, I noticed that the vessel was flying both the Tanzanian as well as South African ensigns.

It was absolutely awesome seeing a South African navy vessel literally on our doorstep! Our hotel staff were in awe at seeing a navy vessel of this size before their very eyes.

In excitement, I called Wolf and Stan over and suggested we must hop on our boat and welcome them, which we duly did.

Pulling up up close to the vessel, I called out and welcomed them, saying that we were fellow South Africans, and invited them to come on land and have a couple beers with us.

A little while later, two semi-rigid inflatable crafts pulled up on the beach. Twelve guys, including the commander, jumped off and came up to the hotel, where they were warmly greeted by everyone.

In typical South African tradition, we had a braai (B.B.Q.) on the beach with the boys and listened intently to their experiences and stories. They told us that President Mkapa had requested the South African navy to participate in a joint "exercise" (a sugar coated word for operation) with the Tanzanian navy over the next couple of days. The commander went on to say that they were one of two frigates from South Africa, the second still on its way up the coast.

I must say that the president certainly pulled out all the stops on this one!

We couldn't stop laughing when they told us of their so called "exercise" together with the Tanzanian navy, earlier that day. The Tanzanian navy vessel – which comprised of a barge, only just managed to leave port before it ran out of diesel. That was the extent of their "exercise" together!

A couple of weeks later, I was summoned to the Tanzanian naval base. When I arrived, I was taken to an old hanger and saw enormous piles of diving equipment, such as masks, snorkels, fins, scuba tanks, wetsuits, etc. There were also other things like refrigerators, dhows, outboard engines, generators, pick-up trucks, nets, oars, anchors and ropes, lying in heaps all around the hangar.

He said that a large amount of dynamite and detonators were also seized. Upon further investigation, the serial markings on the explosives indicated that they were issued to the marine police for the purpose of destroying old ships out at sea. This resulted in several policemen and high-ranking officers being arrested.

The naval officer said that all this stuff had been confiscated as arrests were made relating to the dynamite-fishing practices. Due to the fact that locals couldn't afford to purchase any of the diving gear, he asked me to look through everything to see if I could identify any of the equipment belonging to our scuba center.

Knowing for a fact that nothing from our scuba center was missing or reported stolen, I quickly answered, *"This won't be necessary sir. We check and service all our scuba equipment on a daily basis and haven't found anything to be missing."*

I was absolutely amazed by the huge amount of stuff that cluttered the hanger floor. This had indeed been a massive operation!

"Sir, I wish to thank you and your staff for the huge effort that you've put into this operation. If you don't mind, I would like to get the media out here to take some pictures and interview you on the outstanding job you've done?"

(By this time, my reputation had done its' rounds and everyone knew me as mister Mac.)

"Absolutely, mister Mac!" he eagerly replied!

Needless to say, a nationwide media frenzy ensued. The huge number of arrests and equipment seized resulting from the illegal dynamite-fishing practices made headlines on every TV news channel and front pages of newspapers covered the story for weeks to follow.

Our N.G.O. "M.A.C.T." received two awards for our contribution towards putting an end to the dynamite-fishing. The first award was: "Year of the Ocean" and the second, "Year of the Reefs".

Besides receiving these awards, our business did phenomenally well, due to all the symposiums and conferences which M.A.C.T. held at our hotel. Moreover, the biggest reward of all was seeing dolphins, humpback whales and turtles returning close inshore again.

One day around mid-morning, we noticed a huge crowd of locals walking along the beach towards the hotel.

"*What the hell is this all about again?*" I exclaimed to Wolf, who was standing next to me.

"*It beats me if I know,*" he replied.

As they got closer, I recognized the elders from the village who had previously come to see us.

With the assistance of one of our staff members translating for us, an elder spoke up and said, *"Jambo, bwana* (Swahili for hello sir), *mister Mac, you have kept your promise. The people from the village have come to thank you for ending the killing of our fish. The fishermen can go out every day and come back with baskets full of fish again. We are deeply indebted to you, mister Mac."*

"Hakuna matata, bwana (meaning: no problem sir), *there is no debt. We all make our living from the ocean and it is our responsibility to look after what the gods have bestowed upon us."*

Led by the elders, the locals came one by one and shook our hands saying, *"Asante sana, bwana"* (translated from Swahili it means: thank you very much, sir)

Wow, that was a very touching and exhilarating moment, if there ever was one!

Whilst Denise, Wolf, Stan and Sheryl were all standing on the beach together, I turned to them and said, "*Hey guys, seeing that it's Tuesday, why don't we go out tonight and have some fun?*"

The American embassy showed movies for the expats at their outdoor basketball court every Tuesday evening. In typical American tradition, they also served hamburgers, hotdogs and beer, making it an absolute treat.

That evening, we all excitedly jumped into the car and took off for the embassy. When we arrived, we had to show our passports at the main security office, in order to enter the embassy compound. As we passed through, we gathered in a small group as we waited for everyone to be checked through.

"*What's taking Stan so long?*" I enquired of the others.

After waiting several more minutes, I went back inside the security office to see what the hold-up was.

As I entered, I saw Stan standing behind the counter with his hands in handcuffs behind his back.

Being absolutely perplexed, I asked one of the officers behind the counter what the problem was.

He informed me that when they entered his name in the computer, a notice came up that he was wanted by INTERPOL.

"*What the hell for?*" I asked.

"He has two warrants for his arrest; one for smuggling diamonds and the second for escaping from custody."

I couldn't believe my ears.

I asked the officer if I may have a quick word with Stan.

"You've got five minutes, sir," the officer replied and brought Stan closer to the counter.

"W.t.f. is all of this about mate?" I asked Stan, in disbelief.

With a very sheepish look on his face, he replied, *"I checked out of Zimbabwe and whilst I was busy checking in at the border post in Zambia, they found uncut diamonds in a satchel that was on my bike."*

"Where did you get the diamonds from?" I shot back at him.

"I bought them in Zimbabwe."

"So what happened then?" I wanted all the details.

"They immediately took me into custody. There was no way that I was going to be locked up in a prison in Zambia, so I quickly came up with a plan. Before they could process me, I told them that I urgently needed to go to the bathroom. They pointed to a door behind the counter and told me to go in there. I closed the door behind me and that's when I noticed a small window above the toilet. Without thinking twice, I stood on the toilet and wormed myself through the little opening."

"How the hell did you manage to get away, Stan?"

"I ran around the corner, jumped on my bike and just took off as fast as I could."

"Where did you go to from there?"

"Well, I couldn't stay in Zambia, so I just kept on going until I reached the Tanzanian border post. I knew that they were probably going to arrest me if I tried to exit Zambia, so I had to come up with another plan. I saw a big safari overland truck busy pumping diesel near the border post, so I approached the driver."

"You've got a minute left," the officer chipped in briskly.

"I told the driver that I had problems with my motorbike and asked if he wouldn't mind taking me and my bike across the border on his truck into Tanzania, where I can get it repaired. He could see that I was bull sh*tting him, so he said if I pay him two hundred dollars he would take me across the border without a problem."

Intrigued by his story, I asked, *"So how did you make it across?"*

"I said to this guy that two hundred dollars was too much and that I would give him a hundred once I safely made it across the border. He said that he needed a hundred dollars up-front as a bribe, so that the customs official wouldn't check his truck. The second hundred dollars would be for his effort once we made it across. I agreed and gave him a hundred dollars. With the help of some locals, we loaded my bike onto the back of the truck

and he told me to hide underneath the tarp. We finally made it across the border into Tanzania, where he then dropped me and my bike off in Dar es Salaam."

"But surely you knew that you were going to have a problem at the airport when you had to return back to Germany?" I enquired.

"Everything happened so fast, I didn't have time to think. Only once I made it through, did I come up with a possible solution. I immediately went to the German consulate and reported that I was mugged. I told them that my cash together with my passport was stolen. They issued me a temporary passport in order for me to fly back to Germany."

"Stan how come they didn't pick it up on their computers that there was a warrant for your arrest?"

"It was a chance I had to take. I thought if I reported it quickly enough, the Zambian authorities might not have been able to issue a warrant for my arrest in time."

"Your time is up, sir," the officer said and proceeded to escort Stan to a holding cell.

We were all devastated by the events that took place that evening.

In the end, though, things didn't turn out too bad. Stan had to pay a fine and was deported back to Germany. We later heard that Sheryl and David immigrated to Germany, where she and Stan eventually got married. All's well that ends well.

"The measure of who we are is what we do with what we have."

Vince Lombardi

1 0

When an Uninvited Guest Came to Dinner

ONE EVENING, WOLF, Denise and I took a break from the hotel and went to dine out at a little restaurant in town. Whilst we were having our desert, my cell phone rang. From the caller ID on my phone, I could see that it was someone from our hotel calling.

"This is Mac," I answered.

"Mister Mac, this is Johnson, you must come quickly – there is a hyena in the restaurant!"

In total disbelief, I asked Johnson to repeat himself.

"*Bwana, there is a hyena in the restaurant. He make big trouble!*"

"*Johnson, I'm on my way,*" I replied and hung up.

I repeated what he had told me to Wolf and Denise.

"*A hyena?*" Denise asked in disbelief.

" *Yip, that's what he said. We better hurry and see what this is all about,*" I replied.

We hurriedly paid our bill and left.

Whilst driving back to the hotel in my beloved 1963 Series II Land Rover, Wolf asked, "*If it really is a hyena, where in the hell did it come from? I mean, we are hundreds of miles from any wildlife sanctuary, so it couldn't possibly have come from there.*"

"*I personally think that Johnson has perhaps mistaken a rabid wild dog for a hyena,*" I added.

I parked the Land Rover and ran over to the restaurant with Wolf and Denise in tow. As we came around the corner, we saw a large audience gathered outside the restaurant.

Johnson came over to me and said, "*Come see, Mister Mac, the hyena is still inside.*"

Low and behold, there was the hyena – as real as it gets.

I turned toward him, *"Johnson, do you know where the hyena came from?"*

He looked over at one of our waiters, waving his hand and beckoning for him to come closer.

"Hello, Mister Mac," Mohamed greeted me.

"Hello Mohamed, do you know where this hyena came from?"

"He comes from Mister Dowdy's house," he replied.

"Are you sure it's from Mister Dowdy's house?" I asked in disbelief, knowing that Dowdy didn't own a hyena.

"Friend of mister Dowdy go on safari and leave his hyena with mister Dowdy," he replied.

"Okay Mohamed. Run quickly and fetch mister Dowdy," I ordered.

Dowdy was an elderly Englishman who has virtually lived in Tanzania his entire life. I had visited him on numerous occasions and had coffee with him at his house, which was about a quarter of a mile down the road from the hotel. I would often spend hours listening to all his tales of Africa.

Whilst waiting for Dowdy to arrive, I peered into the restaurant, which was an absolute mess and noticed that the hyena had a collar around its neck, with a short piece of rope attached to it. By the look of things, the hyena smelled the food and either jumped onto the tables or it pulled the table cloths

103

off, in order to get to the food. There were broken plates, broken glasses, chairs turned on their sides and scraps of food strewn everywhere you looked.

A little while later, Mohamed arrived with Dowdy in tow.

"Good evening Dowdy," I greeted him.

"Hello Mac," he replied with a smile.

"Mohamed tells me that this hyena comes from your place," I indicated the beast, who was still having a feast.

"This is Jack alright," Dowdy confirmed.

"My friend Bubba, who was going on safari, came over to my place this afternoon and asked if I wouldn't mind looking after his pet hyena "Jack", whilst he was away. Sure I said, as long as he doesn't bite anyone. He assured me that Jack was very tame and wouldn't hurt a fly. He tied one end of a length of rope to his collar and the other end to a tree. Bubba gave me a bag of dog pellets and said that he would see me in a couple days."

"I think Jack must've got a whiff of the lovely aroma coming from the restaurant, chewed through the rope and followed the scent," I said, pointing to the short piece of rope still attached to his collar.

"Sorry about the mess, Mac. Let me take him home, I'm sure he's had enough food for one evening."

Our guests who had eyes the size of saucers, watched in awe how Dowdy calmly walked up to the hyena, picked up the piece of rope and escorted the hyena out of the restaurant, without any issues.

Denise looked over at me and angrily said, *"I don't care whether this is a friend of Dowdy or not, this Bubba character has to be billed for the damages his hyena caused!"*

"I agree. Will you please tally up an invoice and I'll see to it that it's delivered at Dowdy's place first thing tomorrow morning!" I replied.

The next morning, I gave the bill, which came to twelve hundred dollars, to one of our waiters and asked him to please deliver it to mister Dowdy.

A while later, the waiter returned and handed me an envelope. Upon opening it, I read a return bill which stated: *"Live entertainment for two hours @ six hundred dollars per hour, totaling twelve hundred dollars."*

At the bottom of the bill it said, *"I think we're even. Nobody owes anyone anything!"*

And that's how that score was settled...

"Believe you can and you're halfway there."

Theodore Roosevelt

11

Every Dark Cloud Has a Silver Lining

OVER THE FOUR YEARS whilst living in Tanzania, I had contracted malaria more times than I care to remember. The symptoms were so severe that the best fitting description I can think of is that you wish you'd rather die. In fact, malaria is so rife in East Africa, that it claims the lives of hundreds of thousands every year.

One day, after recovering from yet another serious bout of malaria, I decided that I simply had enough. I sold my shares in the hotel and returned to South Africa.

Not realizing that I was so consumed with the operation of the hotel, at the time I took little notice that my marriage was falling apart, before it was too late. After making several attempts to reconcile, Denise and I subsequently got divorced.

Once back to South Africa, I was alarmed to see how the country had deteriorated so rapidly in such a short time. The most significant difference was the extreme sense of security everywhere you looked. All of a sudden, every home had twelve foot walls with either electric fencing or razor wire on top of the walls surrounding the properties. Security gates in front of doors, burglar bars covering all the windows, alarm systems and armed response were mandatory when insuring your home.

Admittedly, there had been petty crimes in the past, such as burglaries, thefts, assaults, drug use and occasional murders and rapes. However, it never warranted extreme security measures to the extent that people were imprisoning themselves in their own homes. Having to adapt to this new "lifestyle" was exceptionally difficult for me to get used to.

Almost a year had passed, when one of my friends decided to hook me up on a blind date. From the moment that we met, I knew instantly that we were destined to be together. Not only did Catherine and I share similar interests, she was an incredibly beautiful woman as well. Her wavy long blond hair, blue eyes and pretty features harmoniously complimented the beautiful aura that she radiated.

We dated for several months before we eventually moved in together. This was probably because both of us had been previously married and didn't want to over-hastily commit ourselves to a serious relationship.

The topic of the sudden escalation of serious and violent crimes, which were taking place daily in South Africa, often came up in our conversations. One day I said to Catherine, *"Why don't we buy a yacht and go on a sailing adventure together, just get away from it all?"*

Due to the fact that Catherine grew up on a farm and had never set foot on a boat before, I was somewhat concerned that the idea of going sailing wouldn't appeal to her. As a result, I suggested that she read the blogs on the internet of people who have become "yachties" and were living full-time on their boats. That way she could get to know the good, bad and the ugly about full-time sailing.

A couple days went by before Catherine came to me and said, *"I've had a good look at this sailing thing and, the more I think about it, the more I can see myself doing it".*

" Well, Babes, I guess we better start looking for a boat then!" I excitedly replied.

The first decision we had to make was whether to get a catamaran or mono-hull? There are pro's and con's to both. Whilst a mono-hull is less expensive, the downside is that you are constantly "heeling" (leaning to one side) when under sail. A catamaran on the other hand is a lot more spacious, does not "heel" and makes for a much smoother sailing experience. The downside is that it costs more to maintain as well as for mooring fees in a marina. Costly marina fees weren't going to be a problem for us, since we were planning to drop anchor in bays and coves, wherever we could. After looking at a couple of

109

mono-hulls, it didn't take much to persuade Catherine that a catamaran was the way to go.

During the arduous task of finding a good, used catamaran that would suit our needs, I enrolled at a sailing school to get my "Ocean Master's Sailing Certification". Not only was this license a prerequisite in order to check-out of port in South Africa, I also wanted to be proficient with all aspects of sailing a yacht "safely" across vast oceans.

We had become rather despondent, due to the fact that we hadn't found our boat yet. Then, out of the blue, a boat broker called us up and said that he'd found OUR boat. Needless to say, we were ecstatic about the good news and couldn't wait to see it!

From the moment that I laid eyes on that boat, I had a sensation of déjà vu similar to the feeling I had when I met Catherine for the first time. We both instantly fell in love with the boat.

So we took delivery of our boat and eagerly started prepping her for the adventures that awaited us. Though we didn't want to be bound by specific schedules and itineraries, we did however decide on making our way to the Caribbean Islands. Having said that, we had to take several things into consideration, before simply heading off into the blue yonder. This is where many people come unstuck and find themselves in situations that should've and could've been avoided at all costs.

One of the cardinal rules is to plan one's voyage according to the prevailing trade winds and currents which changes with every season. With that in mind, we had to plan on leaving South Africa before the end of April, in order for us to head north. This meant that our window of opportunity was very tight and thus had to get everything ready before the trade winds and currents changed direction.

Fortunately, I had gained some valuable experience as crew on the yacht delivery, which made the planning and acquisition of supplies that much simpler. It isn't necessary to stock up for the entire trip considering that one would be stopping over at several places along the way to replenish necessary items. As a safety margin, depending on the number of people on board, it is wise to take some extra dry foods and drinking water which could be rationed in the event of an emergency.

As the days neared for us to cast off, we were brimming with excitement and couldn't wait to embark on our little adventure. There was also a fair amount of nervousness thrown in for good measure. It would be my very first time assuming responsibility of being captain – and it would also be Catherine's first time on a yacht venturing out into the open ocean.

We had a four day window period within which to leave, before the trade winds swung direction. Just as we were about to cast off, the harbor master declined our clearance to leave port. Upon enquiring as to what the reason was, they informed us that no vessels were permitted to leave or enter the port, due to the huge swells in excess of twenty eight feet which were slamming into the harbor channel.

Two days later, we were finally given the green light to leave port. Having said that, we still had to contend with twenty foot swells, which certainly got our adrenaline pumping! The sheer size of the massive swells dwarfed the forty foot boat, as it sailed down one swell and up another. Each time the boat reached the foot of the next oncoming swell, it appeared as if the towering swell was going to engulf the boat. As disconcerting as it was, we were comforted, knowing that our baby was very capable of handling herself triumphantly.

It certainly pays to heed the advice of old-timers who have sailed the seas many times before. They've been there, done that and got the T-shirt to prove it. Taking their advice into consideration, we sailed due west, in order to get away from land as quickly as possible. Contrary to what one may think, the further you are away from land, the calmer the ocean becomes. This is primarily due to the fact that the pressure systems aren't as erratic over the ocean as they are along coastal waters near land.

Like a duck to water, Catherine got the hang of things in no time at all. In fact, on the second day of our voyage she was already standing watch at the helm on her own. She had also become very proficient in maintaining the log book and recording our position on a paper chart, every three hours when we changed watch. I was very proud of her, not only because it was her first time sailing out into the big blue, but moreover that she remained so remarkably calm and quickly adapted to her surroundings.

On the third day of our voyage, whilst the two of us were sitting outside on the aft-deck, we heard a loud bang which sounded like it came from inside the boat. I quickly went below deck to investigate where the sound came from and discovered that the autopilot had snapped off from the tiller pipe which was connected between the two rudders. With the autopilot inoperative, we had to manually steer the boat twenty-four-seven. Needless to say, it placed a huge workload on us, as we had to constantly keep the boat on course manually. It's only then that we truly appreciated the luxury of having an autopilot.

Once we were two hundred miles perpendicular to land, we changed course and headed north towards St Helena Island which was to be our first port of call. The ocean and strong gusts had become noticeably calmer as the days went by. For the first time, I was able to take out my fishing gear, comprising two hand-lines and lures, which I trawled behind the boat. In no time at all, I caught a number of fish in such quick succession, that I had to put my fishing gear away again before I had really got started.

It is difficult to describe in words the inner peace, tranquility and freedom one experiences out in the open ocean. From the moment we cast off, it was as if we left all our worries, concerns and stress behind us. With only the wind in our sails and the boat gliding effortlessly through the water, every moment felt like floating on a dream!

On the fourteenth day of our voyage, as the sun came up over the horizon, we saw land ahead of us. It was truly a glorious moment as we finally made it to St Helena Island. Soon after we dropped anchor and were cleared through customs and immigration, we took off for the nearest pub to celebrate the first leg of our maiden voyage.

Each with a beer in hand, I raised my beer to Catherine's and said, *"Honey I'm truly proud of you, well done!"*

St Helena Island, located almost slap-bang in the middle of the Atlantic Ocean between West-Africa and the horn of Brazil, makes for a very convenient stop-over. At the time that we were there, they were busy constructing an airport on the island. Previously, it could only be reached by ship.

I immediately ordered a new autopilot from South Africa, which arrived two weeks later by ship. In the interim, we spent our time exploring this beautiful island. It not only carried a very remarkable history, but also possessed a certain British colonial charm with its' quaint architecture and cobble-stone roads. Even the "bobbies" patrolling the streets on foot looked eerily similar to their British counter parts. Though St Helena Island has its' independence, it still remains a British colony, much to the relief of the inhabitants, most of whom would otherwise become destitute without the financial aid of the United Kingdom.

We frequented the local pubs so often that the locals started greeting us by our first names. What we found very humorous were the notices that were posted on the pub walls by the police. A typical notice would bear a photograph and the persons' name, banning that person from the pub for "inappropriate behavior".

On one occasion, whilst frequenting a popular watering-hole in town, we met a lovely, elderly German couple who had just sailed into St Helena Island that afternoon. Sharing similar interests, we soon got chatting.

"How long have the two of you been sailing?" I asked.

"We've been sailing for six years already," the husband replied. *"In fact, this is our third circumnavigation together!"*

"Wow, that's awesome!" Catherine remarked.

Being somewhat inquisitive, I enquired, "*What would you say was the scariest experience you have had?"*

This time, his wife quickly chipped in, *"Oh, the first time the boat capsized, it was a terrible experience and a very big mess. There was flour, rice, sugar, cooking oil, pots, pans, cutlery and everything you can think of, was strewn all over the boat."*

Being somewhat perplexed, I asked, "*You mean to say that the boat capsized for a second time?"*

"*Ag, the second time wasn't nearly as bad. We learnt to stow things properly away on the boat, so it wasn't such a big mess,*" she went on to say.

Not believing her ears, Catherine quickly remarked, "*What? You guys capsized twice?*"

"*No, no,*" the husband replied. "*We've actually capsized three times already!*"

"*W.t.f? After the first time that I capsized, that'll be the end of sailing for me there and then!*" I added.

Darn it, one had to admire these peeps for their tenacity!

Whilst I was in the process of fitting the new autopilot, a mono-hull – also bearing the South African ensign, dropped anchor next to ours. The couple and their two daughters looked visibly shaken and worn out.

"*Welcome guys, how was your trip?*" I enquired.

"*Oh my God,*" the woman replied. "*There were times I seriously thought that we were going to die out there. The waves were smashing into the boat with such immense force, that it knocked us off our feet several times. It was so bad that we haven't been able to cook a meal since we left South Africa!*"

"*What route did you guys take?*" I enquired from her husband.

"*From the moment we left port, we sailed due north. Man, I've never in my life been in such rough seas!*" he replied.

"This is precisely the reason why one should heed the advice from old-timers, and get away from land as quickly as possible," I thought to myself.

As they had been battered to hell and back, we invited the family over for a hearty, hot, cooked meal on our boat.

After spending an awesome time on the island, we replenished our stock with fresh produce, topped off our water tanks and were ready to take on the second leg of our journey to Brazil.

"Everyone has inside of him a piece of good news.
The good news is that you don't know
how great you can be!
How much you can love!
What you can accomplish!
And what your potential is!"

Anne Frank

1 2

Caught Up in a Nightmare

AFTER CHECKING OUT the previous afternoon, we pulled anchor and set sail for Brazil early the next morning. The weather and ocean were near perfect sailing conditions, especially as we had the use of our autopilot back again.

Due to there not being very much to do on the boat, Catherine spent a lot of her time reading. I, on the other hand, either played my harmonicas or just pondered about experiences that had happened in my life.

Here is one such experience that popped into my mind at the time: At age twenty eight, I opted to become a paramedic and was employed by a private emergency medical service. Early one evening, as my crew and I dropped a patient off at a hospital, I received a radio call from dispatch that I must urgently respond to a call at my mother's house. No details were given other than that a shooting had taken place.

All sorts of scenarios raced through my mind, one of which being, *"I truly hope it isn't one of my family members who got shot."*

With sirens blaring, I raced to my mother's house as fast as I could.

Upon my arrival, I was confronted with the sight of several police vehicles and personnel at my mother's residence. Still unsure of what was going on, I enquired from one of the police officers as to who got shot?

Not knowing that I was a relative, he replied, "A woman shot her husband. The guy is still inside the house."

I ran into the house and found my mother and sister sitting in the kitchen in a state of severe shock.

"What happened?" I quickly enquired.

With tears in my mother's eyes and blood covering her hands, she replied, *"I just lost it and shot Dan in the head."*

My immediate reaction was to evaluate the situation and render medical assistance.

With my crew in tow, we ran down the passage towards my mother's bedroom. As we rounded the corner of the passage, I saw my step-father lying motionless in the bedroom doorway, with copious amounts of blood pouring from a bullet hole just behind his left temporal area. After checking his vital signs, it was clear that he was already dead and there wasn't any possibility of successfully resuscitating him.

I thought to myself, *"If she intended to kill him, she surely made a good job of it!"*

While the police were going about their business, I consoled my mother and sister in the kitchen.

"So what happened this evening?" I asked my mother.

"My son, this has been coming for a long time already," she replied, whilst wiping her nose with a tissue.

"At first, I found Polaroid photos in his briefcase of him having sex with several other women. Initially, I didn't want to make too much of a fuss about it and just let things ride. This went on for months and months. Today, when I took his suits to the drycleaners, I found more photos in one of his suit pockets. When I got home, I scrutinized the photos properly and that's when I noticed that he had taken photos of himself molesting Chantelle. That's when I flipped!"

I looked over at my sister and asked, *"Chantelle, why didn't you say something long ago?"*

"He threatened me and told me that if I said anything to anyone, he was going to hurt me so badly that I'd carry the scars for the rest of my life. Besides, this wasn't the first time that this had happened. One weekend when mom was away, he took photos while his seventeen year old son raped me in the swimming pool."

Chantelle was visibly shaken up as she relived the horrid nightmares of her abuse at the hands of this man.

"I'm so very sorry that you had to go through this on your own. I so wish that you'd come to me and told me what this pig was doing to you," I replied angrily.

"So, when Dan got home from work today, I confronted him with the photos I found in his suit pocket. He screamed at me and said that if I discussed this with anyone, he would ensure that I'd be left without a penny or a roof over my head. He went on to say that Chantelle wasn't as innocent as she looked. In fact, he said she had enjoyed every second of it! In a fury, he turned and walked towards the bedroom door. That's when I snapped. I opened my bedside cabinet drawer, retrieved my revolver and shot him."

I grew up in a very loving and caring home whilst my father was still alive. Never in my wildest dreams could I ever have imagined that my mother was capable of murdering someone. Having said that, I'm glad I didn't know what this frigging bastard had done to my sister, otherwise I would have been the one facing murder charges.

"Mom, let's back-track here, for a moment. What did Dan mean when he said that he would ensure that you'd be left penniless and without a roof over your head? I mean, when dad passed away, he left you two houses and over three million in cash. I don't get how Dan could manipulate you like that?"

My mother took a deep breath before she answered, *"Mac, it's a lot more complicated than you may think. When your father passed away, I met Dan and fell in love with him. Six months later, we got married."*

"Much to my disapproval!" I quickly chipped in.

"Be that as it may, I still loved him."

Clearing her throat, my mother continued, *"I had just inherited everything from your father's estate and was unsure of how best to invest the money. Because Dan held a senior position at the insurance company that he worked for, he could buy shares at hugely discounted prices as part of his perks. However, the shares would have to be in his name."*

"Mother, please don't tell me that you were stupid enough to give him all your money?" I angrily snapped at my mother.

"It's not just the cash I inherited that I gave him to invest. I also sold both houses and asked him to invest that money for me as well..."

I couldn't believe my ears, *"Frigging hell, mother, what on earth were you thinking?"*

Before my mother could reply, I added, *"Okay, so you gave him all the money to invest. Surely you had an antenuptial agreement in place when you got married, thereby protecting your assets, not so?"*

"Well, that's how he had me bent over a barrel. We got married without an antenuptial agreement," my mother went on to explain.

"Oh my God, mother. That narcissistic bastard walked into your life without a dime to his name. He even took over dad's car because he didn't have one of his own. To add insult to injury, he took your car and gave it to his ex-wife, because SHE didn't have one either!"

I was absolutely infuriated by my mother's stupidity and gullibility.

"So what about this house that you guys are living in?" I asked.

"Dan said because of the inheritance I received, I would have to pay a lot on taxes if I bought the house in my name. As a result he bought it in his name."

I buried my face between my hands in utter disbelief. The more my mother revealed, the darker the nightmare became.

That's when everything hit me like a sledgehammer between the eyes. No wonder Dan could carry on with all his shenanigans to his heart's content, knowing that he had my mother between a rock and a hard place. It didn't take a rocket scientist to figure out that if my mother ever decided to leave him, she would have been without a roof over her head and not a penny to her name. That narcissistic pig certainly made sure of it!

After the police swabbed my mother's hands for gunshot residue, I said to the lead detective that my mother had experienced severe post traumatic shock and that she should be admitted to hospital where she could be observed overnight. He agreed to it and said that he'll come by the hospital the following morning to obtain a statement from her.

My sister, in the interim, had called my mother's parents as well as her sister and told them what had happened. By the time I arrived at the hospital the following morning, my mother's room was crowded with her family standing around her.

As I entered the room, my grandfather unexpectedly grabbed the front of my shirt and slammed me into the wall behind me.

"Why are you doing this to your mother?" he growled in my face.

In a state of utter shock and disbelief, I asked, *"What did I do?"*

With my grandfather's face literally inches from mine, he growled back at me again, *"Why are you trying to pin the murder on your mother? She's given you everything in life and now you're doing this to her? How dare you!"*

I didn't have a cooking clue what he was on about. So I asked again, *"Please explain to me what I did?"*

125

"Don't act like you're the choir boy now. You shot Dan through the open bedroom window and then sneaked the gun into the house, thereby pinning the murder on your mother!"

"Are you f***ing crazy? Where on earth did you come up with such a ludicrous, bull sh*t story?" I barked right back in my grandfather's face!

He shoved his right forearm hard up-against my throat and said, *"Are you now trying to tell your mother that she is a liar?"*

"Get the f**k away from me," I shouted in his face as I pushed him away from me.

"The lot of you are just making things worse for my mother with your cock and bull stories," I said out aloud. With that, I turned and stormed out of the room in utter disgust. I simply couldn't wrap my mind around the idea that my very own mother had turned the tables and blamed me for murdering her husband!

In the days that followed, I sensed that I was being watched everywhere I went. One day I had enough and called the investigating officer on the phone.

"Why am I under twenty four hour surveillance? Am I considered a suspect in this case?" I enquired.

"We have reason to believe that you may be involved in the murder of your step-father," he replied.

I thought to myself that it was time to finally set the record straight.

"From the word go, I've never minced my words in letting everyone know how I felt about this narcissistic piece of sh*t. I've never liked him and he knew it, so there's no mystery there. If my mother was idiotic enough to get married to him, then that was her own doing. She had to live with the consequences, not me!"

After clearing my throat I continued, "*As for the crazy theory that I murdered my step-father, that is absolutely beyond comprehension. For a start, I was on duty and some ten miles away from my mother's house when I received the call from dispatch. So, how on earth is it possible that I could have murdered him?*"

The officer replied, "*Well, that's what we are busy investigating right now. Your story that you were some ten miles away when you received the call doesn't add up.*"

"How's that?" I asked.

"We've driven that route to the crime scene several times and there's no way that you could've arrived there so quickly. In other words, you must've been in close proximity to the crime scene when you received the call. Furthermore, everyone knew that you disliked the deceased and therefore you had a good motive to murder him."

"Allow me to pop your little bubble, sir?" I snapped at him.

Before he could get another word in, I continued, *"For a start, as part of my training as a paramedic, we had to undergo extensive high speed defensive driving courses. Secondly, my crew will also vouch for our whereabouts when we received the radio call. Thirdly, if you have the balls sir, you can accompany me on a test drive to validate that I I'm more than capable of doing the route in the time stated!"*

"You don't have to get cocky with me, Mister Mackenzie!" he snapped back at me.

By this time, I was absolutely livid that I've been implicated in the murder of my step-father.

"Let me add sir, if you did your work properly, then you would've discovered from the forensics alone that my mother did in fact shoot this piece of sh*t. So why are you going on this wild goose chase when you have all the evidence at your disposal proving her guilt?"

Realizing that he was backed into a corner, he replied, *"We're simply doing our job, Mister Mackenzie."*

"Unless you have something concrete that implicates me in this murder, then I suggest that you call your pack of rats off my ass and stop harassing me," I barked at him and slammed the phone down.

I think what angered me the most, was the fact that my own mother tried to throw me under the bus when she knew full well that she was guilty of shooting her husband!

Several months went by with neither of us saying a word to each other.

I was eventually summonsed to give evidence at my mother's court hearing.

"How do I remain impartial at the hearing, after my mother tried to pin the murder on her own son?" I asked myself.

The only way I could possibly do this, was to refer to my mother in court as "the accused" and not as my "mother."

After a lengthy court hearing, insurmountable evidence proved her guilt beyond a shadow of a doubt. When it finally came down to her sentencing, there was a lot of extenuating circumstances that stood in her favor. As a result, she was sentenced to two hundred and fifty hours community service and two years' imprisonment, which was suspended for five years.

I was adamant that I wasn't going to allow this saga to influence the trajectory of my life going forward. My baby sister, who was only fourteen at the time, went for numerous on-going counseling sessions, and is still scarred by this hellish nightmare to this very day!

*"There is a reason for everything.
You just have to embrace it with an open mind,
then awesome things are possible."*

Mac Mackenzie

13

South America, Here We Come

WE HAD AN INCREDIBLE sailing experience all the way to Brazil, with the wind behind us for the entire trip. Our first port of call in Brazil was Recife, which turned out to be an absolute dump. Not only was it filthy as hell, we didn't feel safe for one second. As a result, we only stayed over for one night and decided to move on the following day again.

Looking at the maritime chart, some seventy five miles up the coast, we saw a town called "Cabadelo" which is situated at the mouth of a river. We were told to go just a little way upriver to a small village named "Jacare", where we could safely drop anchor.

We sailed overnight and arrived at Jacare early the following morning.

"Wow" Catherine exclaimed, when we arrived. *"This place is so beautiful."*

After we dropped anchor, we noticed a yacht on anchor near us, also flying the South African ensign. Excitedly, we jumped into our dinghy and went alongside to introduce ourselves.

I called out, "H*ello, is there anyone onboard?"*

The next moment, this eccentric looking couple in their early fifties crawled out from below deck.

Besides the fact that they were butt-naked and didn't give a hoot what anyone thought about it, both of them had dreadlocks with feathers and beads dangling from twisted strands of hair.

"Hey brother, I'm David and this is my chick, Susan," he announced.

"Good to meet you. I'm Mac and this is my girlfriend, Catherine," I replied.

"We just arrived when we noticed the South African ensign on your boat. We're also from South Africa, so we thought that we'd come over and introduce ourselves quickly."

"That's sweet, mate. I can see that we're going to have a good time together," he said, with a broad smile on his face.

With a gesturing wave of her hand, Susan said, *"You look like chill folks. Come onboard and have a drink with us."*

Besides the fact that it was only nine in the morning, I replied, *"Thank you so much for the invitation, but we still have to go and check-in with customs and immigration."*

David quickly chipped in, *"Relax brother, it's Sunday and there isn't much going on today anyway. Let me tune you, it is quite a rigmarole checking in here. But you guys can relax; we know all the ins-and-outs of how things operate around here. Come onboard, chill and have a drink with us."*

Before I could come up with another excuse, Susan reached out and helped Catherine onboard. As I stepped onboard, I got that very distinctive whiff of pot hanging in the air.

"Come park here," David said whilst pointing to large cushions scattered on a rug on the aft-deck.

I have to admit that it was rather comfortable sitting on the large cushions. Above us were "sarongs" which were draped from corner to corner on the aft-deck, providing much needed shade in the heat.

The next moment, Susan appeared with four shot-glasses in her hands.

"Let's celebrate your arrival here in Jacare," Susan said, whilst handing each of us a drink.

With that, David raised his shot-glass and made a toast, *"Prost, may the mosquitoes get drunk and let them be Merry, Jane or whoever they want, but leave us the hell alone!"*

Catherine and I simultaneously threw our drinks back and looked at each other with glazed eyes. Gasping for a breath, I asked, *"Hey mate, w.t.f. was this sh*t?"*

"This is a local drink called Cachaça. It's made from fermented sugarcane juice. Straight from Mother Nature without any preservatives, GMO's or other bull sh*t," David stated with conviction.

"Good God," I thought to myself, *"I'm sure this sh*t will even cure ingrown toe nails!"*

I knew there and then that we had to get our asses off the boat whilst we were still able to.

We thanked them and agreed to meet up the following morning. Catherine and I precariously clambered back onto our dinghy and headed straight back for our boat.

Once we were safely back on our boat, that's when we remembered where we had previously seen this couple. They were at the same marina that we were at in Cape Town. Whilst they were preparing to leave, they topped up with diesel from the bowser in the marina. Only once they were done, did they realize they had pumped the diesel into their fresh-water holding tank and not the diesel tank. This turned out to be a huge operation, as they had to get a special Hazmat tanker to pump the contaminated water from their boat. Trying to get rid of the diesel-odor in the water tank proved to be an even bigger job.

I have to admit that neither Catherine nor I had slept so well since we departed from South Africa. We woke up the following morning feeling very refreshed and ready to take on the world again.

We met up with David and Susan again, who drew us a map, explained where everything was and the procedures we had to follow. First we took a train to the outskirts of Cabadelo and reported to the police station. From there, we took a taxi into the port in Cabadelo and checked in with immigration and customs, which was just across the street from one another. Fortunately for us, we had David and Susan explain the route and procedures to us, otherwise it would have been an absolute nightmare trying to find everything.

Jacare is a small village on the banks of the Paraiba River, where thousands of tourists flock every afternoon to listen to a musical legend, who has been playing the famous "Balero" on his saxophone at sunset for the past twenty years. From the comfort of our boat whilst sipping on cocktails, we had front-row seats, while listening to the Balero at sunset.

We got to meet a lot of other yachties from all over the world, who had also anchored their boats on the river. As a result, we often hung out and did a lot of things together. One of our favorite outings was taking the train into the city called "João

Pessoa" on Sunday afternoons, where live music was played on the square, in the middle of the city.

Anchoring in the river was somewhat of a challenge, due to the ever changing river currents as tides came in and out. The boats constantly dragged anchor, especially at spring tide when the current of the river would easily exceed seven knots per hour. Whilst Catherine and I were sleeping late one evening, we were awakened by a very loud bang.

"What the f*ck was that?" I shouted out to Catherine.

"I think a boat rammed us," she shouted back.

I quickly jumped up and with my flashlight in hand, I ran outside to see what had happened. When I reached the bow of the boat, that's when I saw that a mono-hull had slammed into us. Seconds later, a man and woman appeared on deck in a state of utter shock. Not knowing that it was their boat that had dragged anchor and slammed into us, the guy shouted, *"We just heard this loud bang, what happened?"*

"Hey mate, it looks like you guys dragged anchor and hit our boat. Are you okay?" I enquired.

"Yeah, just very shaken-up, but otherwise we're okay!"

"Start your boat up and reset your anchor again, we'll deal with this in the morning," I said, whilst pushing their boat with my foot away from ours.

The following morning, when we could see what the damage was, I noticed that there was a tiny chip in the gelcoat right on the bow of our boat. Fortunately it wasn't anything serious at all and easily repaired.

During the hurricane season, the majority of yachties hang around south of the Caribbean Islands until the end of October, before heading up north. There are a few that wing it and push their luck, often with devastating consequences.

Having had enough of this scenery for a while, a bunch of us decided to slowly venture north and explore other countries along the way, still remaining south of the Caribbean Islands.

After checking out of Brazil, we set sail for "French Guiana" and navigated our way some thirty miles upriver to a historic little town called "Saint Laurant de Maroni", where we dropped anchor for a couple days.

It was here that the French decided to set up a penal colony in 1852, which is still well preserved to this very day. What makes it worthy of mentioning is that the French imprisoned thousands of convicts here, even for petty crimes such as loitering. The political prisoners were shipped off to the "Iles du Salut" archipelago islands, which include the infamous "Devil's Island", where the French convict Henri Charriere wrote his autobiography "Papillon", from which a movie was made starring Steve McQueen and Dustin Hoffman.

Intrigued after seeing the movie "Papillon", we made our way over to Devil's Island, where the political prisoners were held captive. When we arrived, we noticed that Devil's Island actually comprises of two little islands next to each other. After dropping anchor, Catherine and I ventured off to explore the islands.

It was absolutely mindboggling to see how every path on the islands were painstakingly laid by the hands of the convicts, who gathered rock from around the islands. Moreover, every wall and building was all built using manual labor.

When stepping into the main prison building where Henri Charriere was held in solitary confinement, one couldn't help feeling very emotional and depressed. Each dingy little cell, with only a single bed taking up half the space, was as dark as the night itself. Without even a hint of sunlight entering the dungeon, one can only imagine how traumatic it must've been for those that were held captive here.

The treatment was so harsh, that seventy five percent of the convicts died whilst in prison. It certainly defies comprehension how human beings could be that cruel to one another. This unwittingly evoked very dark memories of the time that I served as paramedic in South Africa.

14

The Necklace and Other Shockers

WORKING THE GRAVEYARD shift, which was from ten 'til six the following morning, I arrived an hour early at the E.M.S. base station, ready to prepare my rapid response vehicle for my coming shift. Sipping on a cup of coffee after completing the equipment check-list, Dispatch called me on my portable two-way radio with a possible cardiac arrest case.

Within minutes of receiving the call, I arrived at the apartment building and hastily made my way up to apartment 314, with all my gear in hand. Surprised that no one was waiting outside the apartment for the paramedics to arrive, I knocked loudly on the door. With no one responding, I knocked again, this time a lot louder.

"Keep your bloody hat on," I heard a woman yell from inside the apartment.

Eventually the door swung open. In front of me was an elderly woman dressed in her nightgown, slippers with big pom-poms on her feet, curlers in her hair and a cigarette dangling from her lips.

"Good evening, Ma'am, my name is Mac. I'm responding to the medical call you placed with the E.M.S."

After taking a drag from her cigarette, she looked over her shoulder and yelled, *"Hey George, the paramagics are here."*

I was choking with laughter. I've been called many things before, but "paramagic" was certainly a first for me!

The apartment reeked of stale cigarette smoke as I stepped inside. Good heavens, I could hardly breathe with the heavy smoke hanging in the air. No wonder poor George had heart problems with all the secondhand smoke.

While I was attending to George who was sitting on the sofa, his wife fell into her "Lazyboy" recliner, took out another cigarette from the packet and lit it with the butt she was puffing on. On the coffee table next to her was a large ashtray which was overflowing with cigarette butts. I've heard of people chain-smoke before, but never in my life have I witnessed anything like this.

I was almost gagging from all the smoke. *"Mam, would you please put out that cigarette? Your husband is having difficulty breathing with all the smoke,"* I pleaded.

She looked at me with utter disgust and snarled, *"It's about time the old fart kicked the bucket; he's damn useless, anyway."*

The ambulance crew arrived not a second too soon. We loaded George up on the stretcher and wheeled him out of the "gas chamber" as quickly as we could.

My uniform stank so much of stale cigarette smoke, I had to go home and change into fresh clothing...

In the months leading up to the first all-race democratic election in 1994, the two main African tribes that supported the African National Congress (ANC) and the Inkhata Freedom Party (IFP), were at loggerheads with each other as to which political party would rule the country.

The wife of the ANC leader, Nelson Mandela, Winnie Mandela was renowned for her questionable behavior and unrestrained militancy, especially towards members of the opposing IFP party. Anyone who was even remotely considered being an IFP supporter was severely and brutally dealt with. This often resulted in people being hacked with machetes and stoned to death.

Winnie, who was known as "mother" of the "ANC Youth League", upped her antics by introducing the infamous "necklace" as a means to deter opposition members from voting for the IFP.

Later that evening, I was dispatched to a "burns" call in the city of Johannesburg. Expecting to respond to a scene where someone had burnt themselves, I was certainly not prepared for the horrific nightmare that was to follow.

Upon my arrival at the address given, I noticed a group of people gathered on the sidewalk outside an apartment building. Initially it appeared that they were warming themselves around a trashcan which they had set alight. Only when I took a second look, did I realize that what I thought to be trash was, in fact, a human torch.

Armed with only a fire extinguisher in hand, the onlookers who were wielding machete's blocked my path shouting *"Bulala wena"* (kill you). I was forced to witness how this person desperately tried in vain to remove a burning tire that had been pulled down over his arms.

As I'm writing this passage, I can still hear his blood-curdling screams for help in my head.

Just then, the fire department arrived and immediately started dowsing the flames, which was already towering some eight feet above him.

At the risk of my own safety, I shoved my way through the group of savages to render whatever aid I could.

Seeing the remains of the tire still holding this person captive, I yelled for the rescuers to bring the "jaws of life" to cut through the smoldering tire.

Due to the severity of his burns, his death was certainly imminent. Without going into too much graphic detail, I administered large doses of Morphine, via endotracheal tube, directly into his lungs, as a means to minimize his pain during his last minutes on earth.

I've been exposed to very horrific scenes in my career as a paramedic, but nothing could possibly have prepared me for something as horrendous as this. The sheer inhumane savagery that I witnessed that evening burnt deep scars in my soul that will remain with me for the rest of my life.

I often asked myself, *"How is it possible that a human being can be capable of performing such a horrific and savage atrocity like this upon another?"*

With the question unanswered, I decided that the time had come for me to end my career as a medic and move on with my life.

"You must do the things you think you cannot do."

Eleanor Roosevelt

15

Vampires and Gun-Barrels

WE WERE ENTICED by our Dutch sailing friends to join them on a visit to Suriname, which gained its' independence from the Netherlands in the mid-seventies. Our destination was some forty five miles upriver, and as a result, a couple of yachties decided against going upriver and moored near the city of Paramaribo.

Though the river is very broad in places and relatively easy to navigate, the water is very muddy, which easily conceals debris floating down river. Due to a lot of logging taking place upriver, it wasn't uncommon to see enormous forty foot logs which had fallen off barges, floating down the river like deadly torpedoes.

After motoring upriver for hours on end, deep into the rainforest, we eventually arrived at an awesome little oasis called "Waterland", tucked away on the banks of the river. Upon our arrival at the small marina, the host warmly greeted us and escorted us to a really beautiful lounge area that overlooked the river. Within seconds, he had us clutching an ice cold beer, which was manna from heaven in the hot and humid weather. Much to our surprise, he appeared moments later with a platter of mouth-watering treats – welcoming gesture at this magnificent oasis in the middle of nowhere.

There were a diversity of yachties from all over the world at the marina. Some came from the USA, the United Kingdom, Canada, Netherlands, South Africa and even New Zealand. As a result, we all congregated at the lounge every afternoon for sundowners and shared stories of our sailing adventures along the way.

Though we had a truly magnificent time in paradise, all wasn't what it appeared to be. From the moment that the sun disappeared, blood-thirsty mosquitoes like little vampires would come out in their droves and ravish your entire body from head to toe. They were absolutely relentless, so much so that they got into your eyes, ears, nose, mouth and any other exposed cavity on your body, which made going to the bathroom quite a challenge.

After spending a couple days at the marina, the mosquitoes became so unbearable that we decided to move on. Catherine had so many welts on her entire body from mosquito bites, it looked as if she had chicken pox!

As we reached the bottom of the river where some of the other yachties moored, we saw one of the yachts being hoisted onto a ship. Upon enquiring what had happened, we were told that the boat had been struck by a bolt of lightning, which had fried absolutely everything onboard. From the top of the mast, down the rigging, engine, batteries, electronics, lights, wiring, etcetera, was all severely damaged.

We were indeed very fortunate, as this could have so easily been our boat.

By this time, we had our fair share of navigating up and down rivers. Whilst some yachties ventured upriver in Guyana, we decided to rather hang out at Tobago, until the hurricane season passed.

As Catherine and I entered the port in Scarborough, Tobago, we were halted by two guys in military apparel brandishing their automatic weapons at us.

Before I could enquire where we should moor our boat and check-in, the one officer rudely barked at us, *"Where is your courtesy flag?"*

I explained that we didn't have one with us and that we would purchase one the moment we go on land.

"You show disrespect to our country!" he shouted.

"I truly apologize and it isn't my intention to disrespect your country. I promise you that the moment we get off the boat, we will get one and put it on our boat," I pleaded somberly.

"Stay on your boat until I tell you when you can get off," he ordered.

"What is the reason?" I enquired.

"Because I'm the boss. When I tell you to stay on your boat, you stay on your boat," he rudely replied.

I turned to Catherine and said, *"This is absolute bull sh*t. Who does he think he is? We're going to drop anchor and then we're going to check in."*

We dropped the boat anchor, climbed into our dinghy and came alongside the jetty.

"Catherine, quickly turn on the video recorder on your phone," I prompted her.

As we were about to step onto the jetty, the same guy came and stood in front of us.

Aiming his riffle at us, he said, *"Where do you think you're going? I told you to stay on your boat!"*

"Who do you think you're talking to? It is our duty to check-in at our earliest convenience and that's what we're going to do!" I barked right back at him.

"Not until I tell you. Now get back onto your boat," he ordered.

"Just so that you know, we're recording all of this on video. Shoot us if you want, but my wife and I are going to check-in now." I grabbed hold of Catherine's hand, stepped past him and just continued walking.

We could still hear him rambling on with the other officer, as we made our way to the immigration office.

I don't know if he called the office up-ahead or not, but when we arrived, we were met with the same abrupt rudeness, *"What do you want?"*

"Good afternoon sir, we've just arrived by boat and would like to check in," I politely replied.

He pointed at some chairs behind us and said, *"You wait here."*

We waited and waited and waited. Forty five minutes went by without being helped. So I stood up and approached the counter again.

"I told you to sit down," he barked at me.

By this time, I had more than enough of this ridiculously rude behavior. *"First a man sticks his rifle in our faces at the port and now we're being treated like utter garbage. What is the matter with you people?"*

Before he could say anything, I continued, *"You know what, we have everything on video and we're going to hand this over to the media for the world to see. So you either check us in this very second or we're off to the media, the choice is yours!"*

"Do what you want," he replied sarcastically.

I grabbed Catherine by the hand and said, *"Let's go."*

A couple of doors down, we found a boat charter company and stepped inside. We met with the manager and explained what had happened and showed her the video Catherine had recorded on her phone.

"This is absolutely unbelievable, I will assist you any which way I can," she replied.

"This kind of behavior has severely damaged our business, to the extent that tourists don't want to come here anymore," she continued.

The manager made a couple of calls and within the hour, we had journalists, photographers and TV camera crew in the store interviewing us and taking our photographs. They said that they would follow up on the story and interview the persons involved as well. We thanked everyone and left.

I turned to Catherine and said, *"I think we've had enough for one day. We've got twenty four hours to check-in, so why don't you and I just chill out this evening?"*

"I couldn't agree with you more!" She replied.

That evening, whilst Catherine and I were sitting at a bar, sipping on a beer, the news came on the TV in front of us with the headlines, *"Breaking News – Tourists held at gun point"*

"That's us!" I called out to the bartender. *"Please turn up the volume?"* – to which he obliged.

They showed the video that Catherine had taken on her phone, which was then followed up with an interview of us. They also interviewed the manager from the boat charter company, who expressed how damaging this kind of behavior was to the tourist industry as a whole.

Unbeknown to us, there had been an "Ebola virus" outbreak in West-Africa. Since we were from South Africa, they automatically assumed that we were infected by the virus. Instead of telling us and dealing with the situation in a professional manner, they opted to treat us like utter garbage.

"You are famous!" the bartender said smilingly.

I turned to Catherine and said, *"Babes, I don't know if we've cooked our goose or not, but we had to do what we had to do."*

With that, Catherine replied, *"Well at least they'll think twice before they act up again, that's to say they still have a job left."*

The following morning, we made another attempt to check in. This time however was a completely different story. From the moment that we stepped into the immigration office, a senior officer came to assist us.

"Good morning, sir, ma'am. On behalf of the department, I humbly apologize for the bad treatment you experienced yesterday. If there is anything we can do for you, please do not hesitate to call on me personally," he said, whilst handing us his business card.

Catherine and I both thanked him and left.

A couple days later, whilst purchasing some supplies at a store, Catherine saw our faces on the front page of the Sunday newspaper. She grabbed my arm and said, *"Look, we're on the front page of the newspaper!"*

In the days and weeks that followed, we were greeted warmly by everyone, to the extent that we felt like celebrities. Even restaurants and bars refused to take our money.

16

When Tragedy Struck

CATHERINE AND I spent a great couple of weeks at Tobago. We made new friends and also had a great time with yachties whom we had met along the way. One thing about yachties is that everyone looks out for one another and is always willing to help, wherever needed.

We also came across many peeps that were sailing with their family and homeschooled their kids whilst sailing. One of the parents would often provide additional lessons for all the children who were sailing with their parents.

As the hurricane season finally came to a close, everyone started making their way north to the Caribbean islands.

No sooner had we arrived at Grenada, did we hear about the awful tragedy that had struck one of the yachties.

I curiously enquired from a group of yachties who the couple was?

"It was David and Susan from South Africa," one of the yachties confirmed.

"We know them," Catherine responded. *"In fact, we met them at Jacare in Brazil."*

"What happened?" I prompted.

"We were all hanging around at Trinidad, waiting for the hurricane season to pass, when David said that they had enough of that dump and that they were going to move on."

"Where to?" I quickly chipped in.

"They said that they weren't interested in going to the Caribbean at all, and decided that they were going to Panama instead. So off they went."

"The weather unexpectedly turned on them and the ocean churned up like a washing machine..." another person added.

"Man, we heard on the UHF weather channel, that the wind was gusting sixty knots, with thirty foot waves. It was brutal!"

"So what happened to them?" I urged.

"Two days later, we heard on the radio that Coast Guard was responding to a Mayday distress call from a sailing vessel. Their rudder had become inoperative and was taking on water. We didn't know who the yacht was at the time. We did however say amongst ourselves, that we hoped it wasn't David or Susan, since they were sailing along the route where the Coast Guard was responding to."

"Due to the fact that Coast Guard didn't have a rescue vessel near that location at the time, they sent out a helicopter instead."

"All that we heard on the radio was that a woman had been successfully rescued, however the man was already dead by the time they arrived on the scene."

"Being anxious to hear who the person was that had died, we called up Coast Guard. They informed us that when the steering became inoperative, they became sitting ducks, with the waves breaking over the yacht, resulting in the boat taking on water. They believe that the male occupant was on deck at the time when a wave washed him overboard. By the time his female partner came to look for him, he wasn't to be found anywhere on the boat. She reported that he always wore his safety harness and tethered himself to the boat. When she looked behind the boat, she saw him being dragged by the rope only a couple of feet from the boat. Although she tried to pull him in, she just simply didn't have the strength to pull his lifeless body onboard. The Coast Guard believes that he had drowned in the rough ocean soon after he was swept overboard.

They confirmed that the name of the yacht was "Day Dreamer" and the persons onboard were David Smit and Susan van Deventer."

Catherine clasped her hands over her mouth, saying, *"oh my God, I can't believe it!"*

"This is truly devastating news!" I added.

"David was really a nice guy. He was always laughing and telling jokes," one of yachties added, with a smile.

"So what happened to Susan and the boat?" I enquired.

"We heard that Susan flew back to South Africa soon afterwards. We also heard that when the Coast Guard went back to the area, they couldn't find the yacht. They believe that because the boat had taken on so much water, it soon sank."

"This is why Catherine and I often practice "man overboard" procedures. We have done it so many times, that it has become second nature to us," I said, whilst lighting a cigarette.

I continued, *"I've experienced people lost out at sea twice already. I suppose that's the reason why I'm so fanatical about practicing M.O.B. procedures."*

Seeing everyone in such a somber and depressing mood, I suggested, *"We still have some of that Cachaca from Brazil that David liked so much. Come on over to our boat and let's have a toot on David."*

17

The Hangover

WHEN DRINKING CACHACA, unwittingly it would often remind me of an incident that took place whilst hiking in South Africa.

There's a vast variety of really beautiful hiking trails throughout South Africa, of which two of my favorite hiking trails are situated in the Eastern Transvaal near the world renowned Kruger National Park.

On one occasion, a couple of my friends and I decided to hike the three-day "Sabi" trail and then follow through onto the four-day "God's Window" trail. We were all really looking forward to hiking the trails and eagerly went about packing our backpacks. I'm not much into dehydrated foods at all, as a result I would pack fresh vegetables, fruit, nuts and a nice piece of steak that I vacuum-pack, freeze and wrap in newspaper that would last for several days.

My friends, who have hiked with me many times before, were very familiar with my mouthwatering culinary habits (which they naturally adopted). We'd have an absolute feast on freshly baked pot-bread, vegetables wrapped in tinfoil and a tender piece of steak tanned to perfection over the coals. A delicious dinner like this would often be accompanied by a nice bottle of wine.

We completed the three-day Sabi hiking trail and eagerly moved on to the God's Window trail, which is situated on an escarpment overlooking the Kruger National Park. The view along this trail is breathtakingly beautiful, as its name aptly describes.

Fortunately, we didn't have to lug tents around with us, as there are overnight rustic cabins along the trails. This meant that we could conveniently pack other luxuries such as miniature plastic bottles of wine and a couple cans of beer. The cabins were well equipped with bunks, cast-iron pots, plenty of chopped firewood and nice showers that rounded off a great day's hike. We'd often leave a generous tip for the ranger "George" and his wife "Elizabeth" who tended to the cabins so beautifully.

Since we finished the third leg of the hike relatively early that afternoon, I suggested that we pay George and Elizabeth a visit at their cottage, which wasn't far from the cabins.

As we approached their cottage, we met up with George who was relaxing in the shade of a large marula tree.

"Hey, George, how you doing, mate?" I greeted him and shook his hand.

George answered with a broad smile on his face, *"Hey, Mac, good to see you back again."*

"How's Elizabeth doing?" I enquired.

"She's doing just fine, thank you," he replied.

"Elizabeth, come see who's here to visit us," George yelled out to his wife, who was busy with some chores in the house.

Elizabeth came out of the house, drying her hands on a dish towel as she walked.

"Hello Mac, what a nice surprise to see you again!" she greeted warmly.

"It's always lovely to see you, Elizabeth"

George and Elizabeth are indigenous folk who have lived in the area for many years already. They are the nicest, friendliest and kindest people I have met in my life.

"I've brought some of my friends along again which you haven't met in person yet," I explained and went about introducing each of them.

"This is Theresa, Rosemary, Andy and Mike."

Elizabeth shook each one's hand as I introduced them.

"Welcome to our home," she said with a lovely smile on her face.

"Come sit here in the shade," George called, pointing to logs which he had cut to form seats.

"Elizabeth, bring these nice people some of that good beer you made."

"What beer did she make?" I enquired.

"Marula beer," George replied.

I've eaten marula fruit a couple of times before, but never had the opportunity to taste the beer made from the fermented fruit. The juicy fruit are the size of a small plum and has a lovely aroma of pears and passion fruit. It's also extremely rich in vitamin C content, four times higher than that of oranges. In other words, it's good for you!

Elizabeth soon returned carrying a tray and handed each of us a large plastic cup of beer.

I took a small sip at first and was pleasantly surprised how good it tasted. Unlike western style beer that generally has a barley and hops taste, this beer was somewhat on the sweet side, with a slight yeast after taste.

"You did a good job with the beer, Elizabeth, it tastes very nice" Rosemary complimented. Due to the fact that we'd been hiking for several days already, our alcoholic beverages had run out and this was certainly a refreshing surprise indeed.

"Thank you," she replied. *"Now I'm going to bake you some marula bread on the fire."*

"Elizabeth makes very good bread," George said, while stoking the fire.

"I've never heard of marula bread before, how does she make it?" I asked George.

"After she makes the beer, she takes the seed and puts it in the sun to dry. When the seeds have dried, she crushes it and mixes it with flour," George explained.

"Yeah, I've heard that the seeds are very high in protein" I added.

Whilst we were sipping on our beer, Elizabeth stood at a small table and expertly kneaded the dough, like someone who has done it a thousand times before.

"George, I brought you a little present," I said, retrieving a pocket knife from my shorts.

161

"Yabonga gakhulu, numzaan," (many thanks, my friend) George replied in the Zulu language.

"Tonight we must celebrate your visit!" George added.

George placed his plastic cup on the tray after taking a couple of big gulps from his beer. This was a sign that we had to follow suit. We all finished our beer and placed our cups on the tray next to his.

It is customary in the Zulu tradition that woman serves their husbands and guests with beer and food whilst they sit back and relax around the fire.

"Elizabeth, bring us more of your good beer" he gestured, pointing to the cups on the tray.

Elizabeth replenished our cups and passed them around to each of us.

"Yabonga, mama" (thank you, my wife) George replied.

As the flames died down to a grey-ash color, Elizabeth proceeded to flatten balls of dough and placed them onto the grey-colored coals. The lovely aroma of the baking bread instantaneously got our mouths salivating.

Within a couple of minutes, the flattened breads were ready to come off the coals. Using only her fingers, Elizabeth placed the hot bread onto plastic plates and handed them out.

"Before you eat, let me put some marula jam on your plates," Elizabeth said as she spooned generous helpings of jam on our plates.

Without the use of any utensils, we quickly observed how George and Elizabeth dipped chunks of freshly baked bread into the delicious jam, before eating it.

After taking a nice bite size chunk of bread and jam, I responded, "*Elizabeth, this is absolutely delicious!*"

The combination of the freshly baked bread, homemade jam and beer was a feast. Elizabeth ensured that our cups never ran empty and that we had enough to eat.

By this time, we had each had at least four cups of beer and could certainly feel the effect thereof. It was definitely time that we made our way back to our overnight cabin, while we still could.

"Thank you Elizabeth and George, for everything, we really enjoyed it!" I said, trying to steady myself as I was getting up.

We greeted them and started making our way back to the cabin.

All of a sudden, my legs didn't feel like they were mine any longer. My brain was attempting to communicate with my legs, but my legs weren't on the same wave-length. They had a mind of their own!

At that point, we certainly looked like the baboons, warthogs, elephants, ostriches, monkeys and other wild animals after they had eaten the fermented fruit lying on the ground. We were no doubt a spectacle to observe, all for the amusement of our hosts. I could hear George and Elizabeth laughing loudly behind us as we tried to find our way home.

It was troublesome enough that we had to find our way back in the dark of night, let alone being totally inebriated. We had tripped and fallen at least a dozen times, whilst trying to navigate our way back in the dark. We finally made it back in one piece and just collapsed on our bunks. To put it mildly, we were toast!

The following morning, as I opened my eyes, it felt as if I had been hit by a freight train. It was the meanest hangover I had ever experienced in my life. Besides the pounding headache, my mouth felt like a pack of boars had slept in it. My breath smelt even more horrendous – to the extent that I had to rush to the bathroom to expel the beast within me.

As I rounded the corner back to the cabin, it sounded like a porn movie playing, with all the moaning and groaning taking place inside. It was clearly evident that my friends were also experiencing the post traumatic effects of the fermented beer that was consumed the previous evening.

"Oh my God, I'm going to die," Rosemary moaned, as she sat up in her bunk.

Looking around the cabin, I noticed that Theresa still had her hiking boots on and her auburn shoulder-length hair was matted, with grass and twigs sticking out from it. I had to take a second look at Andy before I recognized who he actually was. His face was covered in orange colored dirt from falling face down in the dirt whilst crawling home the previous evening. Mike was nowhere to be seen. Being rather concerned about what had happened to him, I looked everywhere, but still couldn't find him.

"Hey guys, have you seen Mike? He's gone!" I called out to the other three.

"What do you mean he's gone?" Theresa moaned back.

"I've looked in the bathroom, around the firepit, in the cabin, everywhere. He's nowhere to be found!" I replied.

I stepped outside the cabin and called out his name loudly, *"Mike! Mike! Mike! Where are you, mate?"*

"He's here!" Rosemary shouted from inside the cabin.

When I came in again, I followed the groaning sounds that were erupting from under one of the bunks.

I knelt down next to the bunk and called out to him, *"Hey, mate, you okay?"*

More groaning and incomprehensible words came from underneath the bunk.

"Mike, come out from there mate, let me help you," I coaxed.

As Mike slowly wriggled out from under the bunk, he looked like he had been pulled through a bramble bush backwards. His body was covered in scrapes, scratches, dirt and dried blood from head to toe.

*"What the f*ck happened to you, mate?"* I enquired.

He replied with more incomprehensible words which I couldn't understand. I grabbed his sleeping bag from his backpack, folded it and placed it under his head.

"I'm going to brew some coffee mate, you'll soon feel better," I said reassuringly.

I soon got a fire going and brewed a pot of strong coffee for all of us.

"The coffee is ready!" I called out to everyone.

Slowly but surely, everyone started gathering around the firepit and were each given a cup of strong, black coffee.

After taking a sip of coffee, Mike murmured, *"It feels like I've been kicked in the head by a mule."*

"Well, it certainly looks like it, mate!" I responded smilingly.

"By the way, how come you landed up sleeping on the floor, mate?" I enquired.

"The bed was spinning so fast, it felt like I was on a merry-go-round. I had to get down on the floor before I threw up," he mumbled.

The lot of us looked absolutely terrible. In fact, we felt worse than we looked!

There's absolutely no way on earth that we were capable of hiking the remaining five miles. Besides, even if we did arrive at our destination, none of us were capable of driving back home again anyway.

End of discussion, we simply had to stay over!

After we each took a couple headache tabs and a refreshing shower, we spent the rest of day just chilling out.

Later that afternoon, George rocked-up at the cabin with two good sized trout hanging from a piece of twine.

"Hello my friends, I brought you some fresh fish," and proceeded to make a fire.

Not long after that, Elizabeth arrived, carrying fresh corn on the cob, a dish of "marogo" (wild spinach), a couple of potatoes and an onion or two.

"Mama Elizabeth is going to make you some good food to make you strong," she said and went about preparing the vegetables.

George and Elizabeth no doubt saw the state we were in the previous evening and took it upon themselves to spoil us with some good wholesome food.

Elizabeth went about frying the onions in a cast-iron skillet, followed by adding some chopped potato, water, Kernels of corn cut from the cob and finally adding the marogo with black pepper and salt.

Whilst the stew simmered slowly on the side, she placed the fish which George had cleaned on the grill.

When everything was ready, she dished up generous portions on plastic plates and handed it out to everyone.

The food was absolutely outstanding!

"George and Elizabeth, you saved our lives today. The food tastes awesome, thank you!" I commented, before taking another mouthful.

Just then, George presented a leather pouch which was hanging around his neck and proceeded to pour its milky contents into plastic cups.

"Please George, no more marula!" I quickly pleaded.

Handing each of us a cup, he said, " *When bitten by a snake, you must treat the poison with poison from a snake."*

Gingerly we each took a little sip. The milky substance had a nice creamy, yet somewhat rich flavor to it.

"What is this?" I curiously enquired.

"Amarula," he replied.

"First we make spirits from the marula fruit, then we add some fresh goat's milk. It's good for you!" he added.

May the truth be told, whilst it was an acquired taste with the goats milk, it certainly took the hair off the dog!

The commercial version of Amarula comprises of distilled marula blended with cream, which is absolutely awesome, especially when drizzled over a choc-nut-sundae ice cream.

Though we thoroughly enjoyed the food and our hosts' kindness, we certainly had had enough marula for a long time to come!

"The best and most beautiful things in the world cannot be seen or even touched - they must be felt with the heart."

Helen Keller

18

A Close Call

AFTER LEAVING PRICKLY Bay where we checked in at Grenada, Catherine and I set sail around the southern point of the island towards St George, which is on the west side of the island.

As we rounded the southern point, I noticed an old rusted ship some distance away that was heading in the same direction as we were. I didn't think too much of it, seeing that the ship was at least a mile away from us.

It is international maritime law that the vessel which intends to pass another from behind, must pass to the right (starboard side) of the vessel which is being passed. Secondly, the vessel which is being passed must maintain its' course until the passing vessel is well clear.

I ensured that we were maintaining our course and that there was more than sufficient space on either side of us for this ship to pass.

The ship behind us just kept getting closer and closer, without showing any signs of altering course. Being on edge with this ship, I tried to communicate with the captain on channel sixteen on the VHF radio to no avail.

Catherine started getting very nervous as this ship was just getting closer by the minute.

"What's this guy doing?" she yelled.

"I've got no idea. After all, there is more than enough space for him to pass us," I replied.

I attempted to communicate with the ship on the radio again, but didn't get any response whatsoever.

The ship, which I estimated being around a hundred foot in length, was directly behind us and didn't show any sign of changing course at all.

I turned to Catherine and said, *"This guy is intent on maintaining his course. I'm going to give way so that this idiot can pass us."*

With that, I steered our boat to the left thereby giving the ship enough room to pass us. Just as I altered course to the left, the ship also steered left.

"What the f*ck is wrong with this guy?" Catherine yelled.

Looking at the ships' ensign, I noticed that it was from Trinidad with a load of old barrels on deck. There were also approximately ten people standing on the deck near the bow.

The cockroach-infested rust can just kept getting closer and closer, to the extent that I could clearly see three men standing in the bridge laughing at us.

I quickly grabbed an airhorn and gave a long blast, which they simply ignored.

"What the f*ck are you doing?" I screamed at them.

Waving my arms, I indicated for them to pass us on our right. They ignored me again and continued straight towards our stern.

By this time, the ship was a mere fifty yards behind us and closing.

"I'm going to alter course to the right and see what this guy's reaction is going to be," I called out to Catherine.

With that, I quickly steered to the right. No sooner had I steered right, the ship also steered right.

"Are they pirates?" Catherine enquired, with tears in her eyes.

"F*ck these guys if they think they're going to ram us or take our boat!" I yelled out.

The ship was less than twenty five yards from us and still kept going.

"They're going to ram us!" Catherine screamed.

I had exhausted every effort to stay clear of the ship behind us. As a last ditch effort, I grabbed the flair-gun, pointed it at the ships' bridge and fired.

The flair hit the windshield of the bridge, ricocheted down onto the deck between the barrels and the people standing near the bow.

With that, the ship immediately steered left and narrowly missed us by a couple of feet.

Within seconds, I had the flair-gun reloaded and ready to fire again.

"Don't shoot, the ship will catch fire!" Catherine yelled at me.

"Hold this," I said and handed her the flair-gun.

I immediately got on the radio and reported the incident to Coast Guard. It just so happened that one of the Coast Guard vessels was in the port at St George at the time I made the radio call. Within minutes, the Coast Guard vessel pulled up next to the ship, forced them to stop and boarded the vessel.

Moments later, we saw them escorting two men in handcuffs off the ship.

When we looked again, a Second Coast guard vessel came alongside us.

"Are you guys okay?" one of the officers enquired.

"We're fine thank you. Just very shaken up by this close call," I replied.

"Just to let you know, the other Coast Guard vessel arrested the captain and first officer who were severely intoxicated. They are being charged for operating a vessel whilst under the influence of alcohol, as well as reckless endangerment," the officer reported.

"We sailed all the way from South Africa and never once did we fear for our lives as we did today. I really thought we were going to die!" Catherine said with tears streaming down her cheeks.

"We're glad you guys are okay. Please let us know if we can be of further assistance," the officer said and handed me his call card.

We thanked them and proceeded to drop anchor outside the port.

As they say in the classics: *"You haven't lived until you've almost died!"*

"Your big opportunity may be right where you are now."

Napoleon Hill

19

The Perils of Sailing through South America

WHILST CATHERINE AND I were hanging out in Grenada, we met an American couple, "Jim" and "Brandy", who were busy prepping their yacht after storing it during the hurricane season. Having been there so often over the years, they knew the Caribbean Islands like the back of their hands.

They offered to show us some of the best places to visit and where to drop anchor. We took them up on their offer and proceeded to follow them to the various islands and coves. One of which was at Bequia Island, which means "island of the clouds." It is part of Saint Vincent and the Grenadine islands – and by far the most beautiful of all.

We dropped anchor in the crystal clear, powder-blue water in the bay of Port Elizabeth. Ensuring that our boat anchors were set properly, we jumped into our dinghies and went about the formalities of checking in, which was an absolute breeze. Another thing that we found very striking was how friendly and helpful the locals were, without being pushy or becoming a nuisance.

Something that we learnt rather quickly from other yachties was to avoid the tourist traps and hang out where the locals ate and drank. We soon found a little place which was situated one block behind the restaurants that cater for the tourists. They made us feel incredibly welcome and treated us to the best cuisine we had had in a long time – not only that, our total bill, including drinks, wasn't even a third of the price of the mainstream restaurants.

Another awesome service the locals rendered was the delivery of freshly baked bread, croissants, bags of ice and laundry service to and from your boat, whilst anchored in the bay.

Of all the islands that we've visited, Bequia is certainly on top of our list.

We had an awesome time on the island with Jim and Brandy, who certainly knew their way around the beautiful terrain. Unfortunately, all good times come to an end and eventually the time had come for Jim and Brandy to return home again, and for us to venture further north.

Having said our goodbye's, Catherine and I set sail for Martinique, which is part of the French West Indies. After a couple days of sailing, we arrived at Sainte-Anne, located at the most southern part of the island.

We were amazed how many yachts were anchored in the large bay. There were literally hundreds of boats from all over the world that had congregated there. Looking around, it appeared that we were the only boat flying the South African ensign.

Being somewhat tired from sailing throughout the night, we decided to drop anchor and rest for a couple of hours, before going on land and checking in.

We had both just sunk into a peaceful little nap, when we heard someone knocking on the side of our boat. I jumped up from the couch in the saloon and went outside to investigate what was going on.

When I stuck my head out the door, I saw that a French police vessel had pulled up next to our boat. They asked us for our boat registration, log book and our passports, which I handed to them. After scrutinizing everything, they said that they wanted to come onboard and have a look around.

"Do we have a choice in the matter?" I questioned the officers.

They simply ignored me and stepped onboard. I politely requested that they please remove their boots, to which they replied that it was part of their uniform and that they weren't going to remove their boots.

Every yachtie takes exceptional pride in the cleanliness of their boats, to the extent that it is forbidden to wear shoes onboard. I was immensely p*ssed off when the officers who boarded our boat showed utter disrespect by not removing their boots, which left black scuff marks wherever they walked.

Five police officers immediately went about searching our boat. They opened every drawer, cupboard and locker on the boat and emptied the contents out on the floor without putting anything back again. There were boat parts, engine oils, filters, clothing, groceries, spare sails, bedding, toiletries, pots and pans strewn all over the floor. They even went to the extent of emptying the contents of our refrigerator and freezer on the floor. Every inch of the boat was scrutinized thoroughly. This lasted for several hours after which they sat us down in the saloon and started interrogating us.

They questioned us as to where we'd been and what the purpose of our visit at each of the various locations was. Some of the places that they harped on in particular were Brazil, French Guiana and Suriname. It soon dawned on me, that these locations were renown for trafficking drugs, hence the extensive search and the interrogation that ensued.

After turning our boat inside out and the relentless interrogation that followed, I reached my breaking point and said to the officers, *"It is obvious that you are searching for drugs. Let me tell you that I'm certainly not such a dumb ass to take such a huge risk. Not only will I get my ass thrown in jail, our boat which is far more valuable than the drugs, will also be confiscated in the process!"*

One of the officers replied, *"We're only doing our job."*

"Don't the French know how to train dogs which can quickly and efficiently search for drugs, without the mess and harassment?" I replied sarcastically.

Just then, a dinghy pulled up on the other side of our boat and I heard a familiar voice call out, *"Hey, Mac, are you guys okay?"*

I looked outside and saw that it was a French couple, "Pascal" and Claudette", whom we had gotten to know in Brazil.

"Hey guys, come onboard," I called out to them.

Whilst stepping onboard, Pascal remarked, *"We saw the police boat here for a couple hours already and we were concerned that something had happened to you guys."*

*"These officers believe that we are trafficking drugs because we've visited Brazil, French Guiana and Suriname. They've searched our boat for hours already and refuse to pack things away again. Besides, look how they've f*cked our boat up with their boots. It's going to take me weeks to remove the black scuff marks"* I said angrily.

Claudette scanned our boat and called the officers out onto the aft deck. I could hear her communicating loudly with them in French.

Whilst this was going on, Pascal turned to me and said, *"You do know that Claudette is a retired judge in France, don't you?"*

"No I didn't," I replied.

"She'll have their asses on a plate in no time," he said sternly.

After several minutes, Claudette called me outside and said, *"These officers have something to tell you."*

"Sir, we apologize for the mess that we made and for harassing you. Please accept our apology?" one of the senior officers pleaded.

Claudette turned to me and said, *"Mac I told the officers that the search of your boat without probable cause was illegal. I also explained to them that you may pursue legal action against them, if you choose to do so. Furthermore, I told them to pack everything away again in an orderly manner to your satisfaction, and that they will be responsible for the cost of having your boat professionally detailed inside and out."*

"How would you like to proceed?" she enquired.

"To tell you the truth Claudette, I'm highly upset! Our privacy was severely violated and they treated us like absolute criminals."

"I totally understand that you are upset. In fact, I challenged them to search our boat as well, since we also sailed to those countries in South America," Claudette added.

"*I think that our privacy has been violated enough already. We'll take care of putting everything away ourselves. I will however have our boat detailed and let them pay for it,*" I concluded.

"*I have the senior officers' call card, so I'll see to it that the police department settles the bill for you,*" Claudette said with a smile.

"*Thank you so much for your help Claudette, we truly appreciate it. Once we've got everything packed away again, we'll get together for a drink soon,*" I replied.

"The power of imagination makes us infinite."

John Muir

2 0

Jimmy's Ark

SPEAKING OF TRAINING dogs – and other animals for that matter, it reminds me of a friend of mine, "Jimmy", who owned a small farm near Durban, South Africa.

When visiting Jimmy on his farm, you'd be greeted by a variety of dogs, potbelly pig, fox, racoon, skunk or ferret and a handful of Billy-goats clambering on top of your car. It was rather overwhelming and even unnerving at first, seeing all these animals racing towards you. But once you got to meet the *family*, they actually became a lot of fun to be around.

You see, Jimmy was quite weird... or shall I rather say *different* from everybody else. From a young age, Jimmy had an affinity for the strangest of pets, like hedgehogs, raccoons, skunks, ferrets, tarantulas, snakes, monkeys – and the list goes on. Whilst other kids would have a dog or cat, it wasn't uncommon to see Jimmy walking around the neighborhood with a strange looking creature in his arms.

As we became of age, most of us pursuing traditional career paths, Jimmy on the other hand gravitated towards raising weird and wonderful creatures as pets. No one ever imagined that he could possibly derive a living from his strange behavioral traits.

This all changed one day, when a pet shop called him up and said that a production company was looking for a *trained* ferret for a television commercial.

It didn't take long before Jimmy became known as the "go-to-guy" for every conceivable creature, to feature in television commercials and movies.

Apart from a few of his pets which were kept in enclosures or cages, the majority roamed freely on his farm and throughout his house. Even sitting in his lounge, one would have to contend with sharing the couch with his pet potbellied pig, rooster and skunk.

There was never a dull moment in and around the house, with all his pets having free reign on his property. As disorderly as it may have appeared, there was certainly a pecking order amongst his pets, as to which pet occupied a particular piece of furniture or spot in the house. Due to the fact that all of the animals lived harmoniously with each other, perhaps the most apt name for his house should have been *"Jimmy's Ark."*

One day I asked Jimmy how he went about training his pets, to which he replied, *"They aren't pets, they're my children."*

Naturally, Jimmy gave each of his *children* a name to which they responded when spoken to. It certainly took some getting used to at first, seeing Jimmy speak to his pets as if he were speaking to a child.

On one occasion, whilst Jimmy and I were sitting on his porch having a beer, a hog came careering around the corner of the house with a baboon on its' back. This went on for a couple minutes before *Cheeky* (the monkey) decided that he also wanted in on the fun. As *Snout* (the hog) and *Freddy* (the baboon) made another round, the monkey jumped onto the hog's back and clung onto the baboon in front of him.

This naturally gained the attention of the dogs (of varying descriptions) lying around, who also decided to join in and give chase.

Just as I thought I'd seen it all, a pygmy donkey and a handful of Billy-goats also started giving chase.

The next moment, Jimmy jumped up and joined the animals running around the back yard making funny animal noises.

I was absolutely bursting at the seams with laughter. Never in my life did I imagine I'd witness anything like this!

187

Unfortunately, this took place at a time when there weren't cell phones handy to quickly take a video. I can just imagine how many millions of hits I'd get on *YouTube!*

As things started to simmer down, Jimmy made a big fuss of each of the animals and gave them all a treat.

"That's how you train animals. They love to play and have fun!" he said.

Surprisingly, his house was spotlessly clean, without any foul odors hanging in the air.

Upon enquiring how he managed to achieve that, he replied, *"All of the animals routinely have their baths, one way or another. Whether it is whilst playing under the sprinkler in the back yard, or physically shampooing them in the tub, they are well accustomed to being groomed since a very young age. Naturally they are all potty-trained and go about their business outdoors."*

"But just like children, one of them will occasionally get up to some mischief and needs to be reprimanded," he added.

"How do you reprimand them?" I asked.

"I take away their quota of beer for the week!" he said with a smile.

His *children* were also very well behaved, for example, you wouldn't see any of them begging for food around the dinner table.

Speaking of food, I asked Jimmy, *"This must surely cost you a small fortune feeding the different animals each their special diets?"*

"No doubt, mate" he replied, *"That's why I charge a small fortune to have one of my children feature in commercials or movies. Besides, it's not easy finding animals that can perform tricks like mine are capable of doing."*

Jimmy was certainly one of a kind. He had this natural knack with animals and the ability to train them to do virtually anything. For example, if a producer required a scene where a rooster would ride on the back of a goat, then he'd train the animals to do exactly that.

Needless to say, Jimmy made a fair amount of money!

"It is by acts and not by ideas that people live."

Anatole France

21

When Things Go Wrong

AFTER WE HAD our boat beautifully detailed inside and out – courtesy of the Martinique Police department, we headed off to St Maarten. It's a peculiar island, in that one half of the island is French, and the other half is Dutch. Depending on which side of the street you walked on, you'll either be on French or Dutch soil.

Seeing that I've been to Oyster Pond on the east side of the island while crewing on a yacht delivery, I decided that it will be a nice place to drop anchor for a couple of days.

Arriving at the channel to Oyster Pond, one certainly had to have your wits about you when navigating the "S" shape channel into the protected pond. Not only did you have to keep a sharp lookout for reefs that protected either side of the narrow channel, the incoming and outgoing tides also created strong swells and currents that added to the challenge.

Several boaters had severely come unstuck, either whilst attempting to enter or exit the channel. On my previous visit there, I had personally seen a mono hull come dangerously close to capsizing when they attempted to exit the channel on an outgoing spring tide. As the tide receded, it drew an enormous amount of water from the pond into the ocean, thereby creating fifteen plus foot swells that boaters had to contend with head-on.

Overlooking the beach and the entrance to the pond is the infamous Oyster Bay Beach Hotel where it is said that Marilyn Monroe and JF Kennedy had a naughty weekend away together.

There are a couple of really great pubs and restaurants on the pond fringe, particularly at happy hour, when yachties hang out together and have a great time. After one too many hangovers, it was time for Catherine and I to move on and experience other places on this beautiful island.

We decided to head south and drop anchor on the Dutch side at Simpson Bay Lagoon, along with dozens of other yachts.

Inadvertently, our timing was absolutely perfect, because it so happened that the Heineken Regatta was due to take place in a couple of days.

As Catherine and I relaxed with a nice cold beer at the St Maarten Yacht club, I saw a note on the notice board stating that they were looking for volunteers to assist with the regatta. Upon further enquiry, Catherine and I opted to volunteer on one of the water taxi's collecting people at their yachts, bringing them to the yacht club and then dropping them off again.

Due to Heineken sponsoring the regatta, all the volunteers were given really nice shirts, caps and other Heineken apparel. A marquee was erected behind the yacht club for the volunteers, where we could drink as much beer as we wanted when off duty. They really spoiled us with great food and a lot of refreshments throughout the day.

The festivities during the regatta were endless, with decent bands playing everywhere you went. They also erected a huge stage on the beach, where top bands would entertain the crowds.

Though it is true that a lot of drinking takes place especially amongst yachties, maintaining your boat also requires considerable effort.

Catherine took care of the interior, which in itself is a big job. Due to the humidity, there is a tendency for mildew to form, particularly inside cupboards, the heads (bathroom) and enclosed areas or spaces. As a result, Catherine had to clean the surfaces with a mixture of white vinegar, bleach and water on a regular basis.

Besides cleaning and polishing the exterior surfaces of the boat, many other things had to be maintained, such as scrubbing down the hull, wiping all stainless steel parts down with a silicone-based lubricant to prevent rust, inboard engine maintenance and servicing, dinghy outboard engine servicing, washing all the lines with soap and water, servicing the batteries, checking all the electrical systems, cleaning the solar panels – and the list goes on. This helps to explain why yachties drink so much beer... We have to keep hydrated!

Unless one had a healthy budget and could afford to dock in at marina's, most yachties, including ourselves, dropped anchor where ever we went. So, if you needed to go anywhere, you had to make use of your dingy. This also meant carting twenty five liter plastic drums of fresh water and diesel to the boat, using your dinghy.

The reason why I'm mentioning all of this is to clear the myth that yachties just lie around, drink all day and have a good time. There is no doubt a lot of work goes into ensuring that your boat is serviceable and in good order at all times. Having said that, breakdowns still occur when you least expect them.

An example of this very thing happened when we were sailing along the east coast of Cuba in what is known as the *Old Bahama Channel*. The tiller pipe that connected the two rudders to each other broke off. Thank God this happened as we exited the channel, just to the north of Cuba.

As a result, we were unable to steer the boat any longer, and therefore were at the mercy of the wind and currents that carried us where ever it wanted to.

I quickly went below deck to see if I could somehow repair the tiller. Being such a confined space, I could barely fit my arms inside and had to resort to very rudimentary repairs, at best. Taking a broom handle which I cut into foot-long lengths, I braced the two pipes together with the pieces of wood and zip-ties.

Knowing that this was only a temporary repair which could fail on us at any given moment, for safety reasons, I opted to put out a *Pan Pan* distress call on the VHF radio. Due to the fact that VHF radios only have a limited range of around seven miles, the only way I could communicate with the Coast Guard was for other vessels to relay my distress call.

Fortunately, a passenger ship which just happened to be in close proximity to us, heard our distress call. They replied by offering to come alongside us and send two of their engineers over to assist us. I thanked them for their most appreciated offer, but said that we weren't in dire straits at the moment. I asked them just to let Coast Guard know of our situation, our current position, number of people onboard and our e.t.a. to Miami, Florida being the closest port to us.

Minutes later, the passenger ship notified us that they had communicated with Coast Guard, who in turn said that they had us on radar and would keep an eye on us.

My rudimentary repair held well, to the extent that we could make it to the port in Miami, where we had the tiller repaired.

Throughout our sailing experience, we were absolutely amazed at the way everyone looked out for each other and were always willing to render assistance.

2 2

The Haunted Hospital

CATHERINE AND I were sitting around chatting one afternoon, when she asked me, *"By the way, how did you get that scar on your arm?"*

Looking down on my left forearm I replied, *"Early one evening, while I was riding my motorbike, I entered a "S" bend in the road, when all of a sudden I saw headlights of a vehicle right in front of me on my side of the road. The vehicle was so close that I had to make a split second decision how I was going to react. Had I remained upright on the bike, the vehicle would crash into me head on and I'd be killed. The only option was to slam on the rear brake and allow the bike to skid out from under me.*

This resulted in the bike being wedged under the front of the vehicle, with me sliding on the asphalt behind it. This quick action no doubt saved my life; however it left me with road rash all down the left side of my body, of which my left forearm was the worst."

I took a sip of my drink and continued with my story, *"An ambulance arrived and took me to the Kempton Park Hospital, which happened to be one of the top hospitals in South Africa at the time. After a very painful ordeal in the E.R., where they scrubbed my wounds in order to remove the debris, I was sent to a ward for observation, until the next day."*

"Ouch, that must've hurt like hell!" Catherine exclaimed.

After lighting a cigarette, I replied, *"I'll have sutures any day compared to road rash!"*

"So there I was in a ward with two other guys, feeling very sorry for myself. I looked over to the guy to the left of me and asked what he was in for? He replied that he just had his appendix removed earlier that afternoon. He went on to say that he had a very weird experience whilst being in theater."

"Tell me about it, mate" I urged him.

I could clearly see that he was very disturbed and shaken up from his experience.

"Man, I don't know how to tell you this? It was truly a horrific experience," he began.

"I remember lying on the operating table with a drip in my arm, and seeing the anesthetist administering a drug into the drip. Shortly afterwards, I started sinking into a deep sleep. Sometime later, whilst they were operating on me, I felt someone tugging on me in a weird kind of way. It's as if I was trying to resist, but the tugging just became more and more aggressive."

He sat up and coughed before continuing, *"The next moment, I felt myself floating above my body, looking down at everyone around me on the operating table. I could clearly see the doctor removing my appendix and saying to the theater sister that they got it just in time before it burst."*

"So it was like an out-of-body kind of experience?" I confirmed.

"Yeah mate. But it just got worse..." clearing his throat, he continued.

"The next moment I felt myself floating swiftly through dark corridors and hearing doors slamming closed around me as I went down a dark passage. I also heard several voices screaming, 'Help me, help me,' as I went by."

"All of a sudden, I was on top of the hospital roof, looking around me. I remember seeing a smoke stack or chimney kind of thing behind the hospital, which resembled a crematorium."

I could see that he was really troubled by his experience, as he continuously repositioned himself.

"F*ck, mate, the next thing I felt a hard push from behind, which caused me to fall forward onto the edge of the roof. I looked down the side of the building and saw a pair of blue sneakers with white laces lying on a narrow ledge a floor below me. Just then, I felt someone or something trying to shove me off the roof. I fought back with all my strength and I remember shouting, "I'm not going to die!"

"Immediately thereafter, I saw myself looking down in the operating theater, with the doctor and nurses hurriedly busy around my body. The next thing I remember was waking up in the recovery room, with a doctor at my bed asking me if I'm feeling okay?"

"I was still feeling rather groggy from the anesthesia, as the doctor told me that my heart stopped whilst they were operating on me – and they had to resuscitate me."

"Wow, what an experience, mate!" I exclaimed.

He looked over at me and said, *"It was terrifying – to put it mildly."*

"Do you think that he might just have had a horrible dream?" Catherine questioned.

"Well that's exactly what I thought might have happened. However, the specifics in his account of what had happened were troubling me to the extent that I couldn't wait for the sun to rise the following morning, so that I could check things out for myself," I replied.

After taking another sip of my drink, I continued, *"So, early the next morning, whilst clothed in a hospital gown, I decided to go and do some exploring. The ward that I was in happened to be on the fourth floor. So I walked up a flight of stairs to the fifth floor and made my way down a long passage, towards the back of the hospital. Upon reaching the end of the passage, I opened a window and looked down the side of the building to see if I could find the pair of sneakers that this guy mentioned in his account of things, but I couldn't see anything. As I looked up, I noticed the smoke stack of the crematorium behind the hospital."*

"That's what he said he saw whilst being on the roof, not so?" Catherine enquired.

"Well that's exactly what I thought. But then again, he could have seen it from the street as well and it may have just been something which was in his subconscious mind when he dreamt about it. Still not too sure about the whole story, I decided to go up to the sixth floor to see if I could find anything there. When I got there, I looked out the window and there was the pair of blue sneakers with white laces on the ledge exactly as he saw in his account of what happened."

"You've got to be kidding me!" Catherine exclaimed.

"There it was in broad daylight. This was absolute proof that this guy had an out-of-body experience whilst being in the operating theater. Besides, there weren't any windows directly above the area where the sneakers were lying. So how did it get there?" I pondered.

"I don't believe in ghosts or anything like that, but this is really weird and creepy," Catherine added.

"When I got back to the ward, I told this guy what I had seen."

"I knew this wasn't a dream. It felt so real and vivid that I never doubted what I had experienced," he affirmed.

I later heard of several other people, including staff, who had terrible experiences at that hospital.

Three years later, on December 26th 1996 to be precise, the hospital closed its doors. Not a single thing was removed from the hospital and transferred to another hospital or facility. Even the patient files, beds, furniture, wheel chairs and the like were left behind.

23

The Bucket List

SOME 8, 500 MILES later, we finally arrived in Fort Lauderdale Florida, where we decided to sell our boat and trade it in for a caravan (R.V.) to tour through the United States. But that is another story entirely!

Although we hadn't circumnavigated the planet or set any records of any kind, the fulfillment and sense of accomplishment we gained from our sailing adventure, has been a major personal achievement in our books.

Most importantly, I am incredibly proud of Catherine, who for the first time in her life set foot on a boat and sailed halfway across the world. *"Well done to you, girl!"*

Subsequently, whenever Catherine goes through tough or challenging times, she draws energy from this experience, which in turn supplies her with the necessary strength and tenacity to see things through.

Here is a fact of life: "You are going to die! We all have a limited time on earth. You might die tomorrow or decades from now, but eventually you will die."

So the question is what are you doing *today* with the limited time that you have on this earth?

The answer to that question is to make a list of things that you'd like to accomplish before you kick the bucket. Hence the term: "Bucket List."

I personally believe that everyone should have a bucket list of their own. It doesn't necessarily have to be off the wall or stupendously adventurous, as long as it is something to strive towards and provides reasons for living a life fully lived.

There are many reasons why people battle putting a bucket list together, excuses such as *I'm too old or I'm too young, I don't have enough money, I have a family, my children are too young, I don't have enough time, I'm not adventurous,* and the list goes on.

Unfortunately, many people have surrendered to their subconscious beliefs that some or most of the above is true. I have news for you – it's all a myth. You can do anything that you put your mind to!

HERE ARE SOME EXAMPLES:

IRENE O'SHEA, at the age of 102, made history as the oldest person to skydive, jumping out of a plane at 14,000 feet in South Australia.

THE YOUNGEST PERSON to skydive was Toni Stadler from South Africa, who, at age 4, performed a tandem skydive at 10,000 feet.

BUDHIA SING WAS the youngest person to finish a marathon. By age 4, he had completed 48 marathons.

EVE FLETCHER, AT AGE 75, is one of the oldest women still surfing.

80 YEAR OLD YUICHIRO Miura, from Japan, became the oldest person to scale Mount Everest.

JEROME DE FREITAS at age 101 is still a professional skateboarder.

"WHAT'S ON YOUR BUCKET LIST?"

There are several types of activities that you can add to your bucket list. To help you create your own unique bucket list, go through the categories below and check the boxes on the left of the activity you'd like to do. Once you've accomplished your goal, return to your bucket list and check that item off in the box on the right. If you don't find a particular activity listed below, you can add your own activity in the spaces provided.

HUMANITARIAN AID is one of the most fulfilling activities that everyone should have on their bucket list of things to do. Take a look at the following categories and the activities I have suggested, and then be brave enough to add your own!

✓	Humanitarian Aid	✓
	Give a total stranger food	
	Volunteer at a animal shelter	
	Contribute a monthly donation towards a charity organization	
	Volunteer at your local community center	
	Volunteer at your local soup kitchen or shelter	
	Become a FEMA reservist	
	Enroll in a first aid course	
	Take a CPR class	
	Volunteer your skills for disaster relief programs	
	Volunteer at your local fire department	
	Become a disaster rescue volunteer (www.primalsurvivor.net)	

✓	Hobbies	✓
	Learn how to sketch	
	Learn how to paint	
	Learn how to play a musical instrument	
	Join a dog training club	
	Take up photography	
	Write short stories	
	Enroll in a cooking/baking course	
	Enroll in a pottery class	
	Learn how to do leatherwork, decoupage, scrapbooking	

✓	Travelling	✓
	Watch the sun rise (east) and sunset over the ocean (west) on the same day in Florida	
	Backpack through the USA	
	Backpack through Europe	
	Travel across the USA from coast to coast by train (www.amtrak.com)	
	Hire a sailboat in the Caribbean Islands, barefoot or with a captain (www.sunsail.com)	
	Take a safari in Tanzania or Namibia, Africa (www.tourradar.com)	
	Visit the "Burning Man" festival in Black Rock City, Nevada (www.burningman.org)	
	Take a transatlantic cruise onboard the Queen Mary 2	
	Swim with the pigs of Exuma Island, Bahamas	

✓	Adventure	✓
	Learn to skydive or tandem jump	
	Learn how to paraglide	
	Learn how to fly microlights, light aircraft, helicopters	
	Go bungee jumping	
	Dive the Great Barrier Reef, Queensland, Australia	
	Go ziplining	
	Swim/dive with dolphins (www.dolphinaris.com)	
	Learn to scuba dive (www.padi.com)	
	Enroll in a fire walking class	
	Go whitewater rafting/kayaking	

"You only live once, enjoy the ride!"

About the Author

With Mac, there is never a dull moment! Being a typical South African, he makes his own biltong (beef jerky... just better), and braai (B.B.Q.) as often as the weather permits. He loves to cook spicy Indian curry dishes or seafood cuisine.

Mac and his wife live in Florida, love to travel and explore little remote places off the beaten track in their caravan (RV). With his new book, "Never a Dull Moment" barely out of the stables, he's already drumming up his second book, which promises to be quite a scream, as he reflects on their journey across the United States in their RV. No doubt there are some wild tales to be told!

Be sure to say hi on Facebook or shoot him an email, he would love to hear from you!

Email: macmackenzie47@gmail.com

Thank you for purchasing my book...

Much appreciated! Please be so kind as to leave a

review on my website: **www.LiveBoldly.me**

As a gesture of my gratitude, I will send you a FREE

electronic copy of my "Success Tool kit."

Acknowledgments

This book would never have seen the light of day without the help of two special ladies:

CHRISTINE BEADSWORTH did an amazing editing job with my rudimentary manuscript. She went above and beyond what anyone could expect from an editor.

Thank you Christine!

NICOLE BARTELS blew my mind with her extraordinary talent when it came to designing the cover.

Thank you Nicole!

Made in the USA
Coppell, TX
30 November 2020

42478333R00125